MYTHS
AND
MEN

MYTHS
AND
MEN

Patrick Henry
George Washington
Thomas Jefferson

BERNARD MAYO

HARPER TORCHBOOKS
The Academy Library
HARPER & ROW PUBLISHERS
NEW YORK, EVANSTON AND LONDON

MYTHS AND MEN

© Copyright 1959 University of Georgia Press

Printed in the United States of America.

Eugenia Dorothy Blount Lamar Memorial Lectures, 1958. Delivered at
Mercer University on November 19 and 20.

This book was originally published in 1959 by the University of Georgia
Press, and is here reprinted by arrangement.

First HARPER TORCHBOOK edition published 1963 by
Harper & Row, Publishers, Incorporated
49 East 33rd Street
New York 16, New York

Library of Congress Catalog Card Number: 59-10512.

FOR PEGGY

Contents

Foreword

THIS SECOND SERIES OF THE EUGENIA DOROTHY BLOUNT LA-mar Memorial Lectures was given at Mercer University in November, 1958. The Lamar Lectureship, established in 1957, was made possible by a bequest to Mercer University from the late Mrs. Lamar, who requested that income from the endowment should be used "to provide lectures of the very highest type of scholarship which will aid in the permanent preservation of the values of Southern culture, history, and literature."

As a leader in the cultural life of the South for nearly three-quarters of a century, Mrs. Lamar was greatly concerned with perpetuating the values of her Southern heritage and emphasizing the role of these values in American history. The establishment of the Lamar Lectureship at Mercer University was in keeping with Mrs. Lamar's far-sighted philanthropy, catholic taste, and enlightened patriotism. Because of these traits of a noble character, expressed so typically in the Lamar bequest, Mercer University cherishes the memory of this distinguished Southern gentlewoman who spent her early years in the shadow of the University from which she received the honorary degree Doctor of Laws.

The selection of Bernard Mayo, a leading American historian and exponent of the biographical approach to history, as the second Lamar Lecturer would have pleased Mrs. Lamar. Like her, he possesses a love of the American past in all of its sectional aspects that enables him with his unique literary artistry and penetrating historical scholarship to sift the golden grain of truth from the chaff of myth in evaluating the seminal influence of three great Southerners—Washington, Henry, and Jefferson—as shapers of the American tradition.

MALCOLM LESTER, *Chairman*
The Lamar Lecture Committee

Mercer University
Macon, Georgia

Preface

THE ROLE OF HISTORIAN-DETECTIVE ASSUMED IN THESE LEC-
tures stems from years of teaching history through biography and from some chance remarks by William Faulkner
and Nancy Hale. When honored by the invitation of the
Lamar Lecture Committee I began to mull over possible
topics dealing with Southern history-makers. Mr. Faulkner
by referring to the Old Dominion as "the mother of all
the rest of the South" confirmed my idea of talking on
these three Virginians: Patrick Henry, George Washington, and Thomas Jefferson. My decision to report on them
as myths and as men took shape from Miss Hale's casual
remark contrasting the image of Jefferson she had in her
New England girlhood with the image of him she found in
a Charlottesville permeated with Jeffersonian hero-worship.

These case histories in hero-worship, miniature critical
studies in reputations, are presented with all the limitations of the lecture form. Though brief, they may encourage a more realistic approach to men and events of the
present as well as the past. All three cases abundantly illustrate the uses and abuses of history. All three reveal how
the flesh-and-blood men, humanly fallible yet with the

inspiring qualities of greatness, have been distorted and obscured by conflicting interpretations and by myths that defame and myths that glorify. Their images bright and dark are here noted. The men themselves are evaluated. And some attention is paid myth-makers, idolaters, and iconoclasts, such as William Wirt, Timothy Pickering, Gertrude Stein, and the ineffable Parson Weems, who in his own fashion aspired "to *Enlighten,* to *dulcify* and Exhalt Human Nature—by GOOD BOOKS."

The art of biography has noticeably matured since the Parson's day. But the Weemsian tradition is still with us. However disguised, it continues to disregard Virginia Woolf's dictum that biography should always fuse the rainbow of personality with the granite of truth, "truth in its hardest, most obdurate form." I was given the opportunity to make this and other observations in an informal talk on the biographical approach to history which served as an introduction to these Lamar Lectures. That initial meeting with students and faculty who were so flatteringly responsive and intellectually stimulating is one of many pleasant memories of the visit to Mercer University in November of 1958. Mrs. Mayo and I were most generously entertained in Macon by Dean and Mrs. Malcolm Lester, Mrs. Peyton Anderson, and other warmhearted Georgians. We met old friends, made new ones, and came away convinced that the proverbial hospitality of Middle Georgia is definitely not a myth but a dulcifying reality.

BERNARD MAYO

University of Virginia
Charlottesville, Virginia

LECTURE

ONE

The Enigma of Patrick Henry

IT WAS VERY COLD THAT FEBRUARY 22ND IN 1858 WHEN VIR-
ginians in Richmond's Capitol Square proudly unveiled
Thomas Crawford's equestrian statue of George Washington and his standing figures of Thomas Jefferson and
Patrick Henry. Yet for hours, as snow flakes continued to
fall, thousands of patriotic pilgrims from all parts of
America were warmed and enraptured by the honors extravagantly paid these heroes according to the text long
ago prescribed in Ecclesiasticus: "Let us now praise famous
men and our fathers that begat us." In glorifying them as
The Sword, The Pen, and The Trumpet of the Revolution, orators and poets tended to enhance them as myths
and obscure them as men. In these "mystic rites" of
patriotism Washington was the deified Father of His
Country, to whom Crawford had carved "not merely a
monument . . . but an altar erected to Heroic Virtue
itself." Fervent, though briefer and less mystical, were the
tributes to Jefferson, "the greatest political genius," and to
Henry, the unrivalled " 'Homer of orators' whose mighty
voice comes ringing down the ages . . . with those watch-
words of civil revolution and progress, 'Give me Liberty
or give me Death!' "

All three great men so fulsomely eulogized a century ago
are today, as they were then, vitally a part of our living
American heritage. Yet today, even more than in 1858,
they have been so long uncritically praised, and dispraised,
that all three are heavily myth-encrusted. Each presents a
formidable challenge to the historian-detective who would
separate the flesh-and-blood man from the obscuring
legend. Of the trio Patrick Henry is by far the most perplexing for anyone who would critically compare his
popular image with that presented by scholars, with their
varying and often sharply conflicting interpretations. For
the more one probes into his strange case the more one is
reminded of Sir Winston Churchill's remark about Russia:
"It is a riddle wrapped in a mystery inside an enigma."

This may seem surprising, since Patrick Henry as a folk-
hero is well established in the popular mind. A recent
Gallup poll on quotations from our history revealed that
48% of Americans know him as the author of those ever-
inspiring words "Give me Liberty or give me Death!"
Though topped by the 61% who know that Mae West
said "Come up and see me some time," he fared better
than Lincoln, Wilson, and the two Roosevelts. Evidently
his classic speech of American liberty, reprinted countless
times ever since it appeared in William Wirt's pioneer
biography of 1817, is still being declaimed by countless
American schoolboys. Yet what is history to the scholar is
not always the same thing to the public. There are ele-
ments of truth, of course, in the popular image of the man
Lord Byron called "The Forest-born Demosthenes." But
knowledge of Henry is usually confined to his Liberty or
Death speech, the main prop of his popular fame, and to
his Treason speech. Relatively few Americans know that
the authenticity of both speeches has been questioned, or
that historians disagree as to many aspects of his character
and career. In the public mind a few vaguely-known facts

are with wishful fancy blended and blurred into myth, as is the case of all folk-heroes.

This is peculiarly true of Patrick Henry, since, more than most American heroes, he is largely the product of reminiscences, the very stuff of myths, always suspect because of the lapses and tricks of memory. He left behind him so few letters and recorded speeches, so little source material, that his story must be reconstructed from what his friends and, alas, his enemies had to say and write about him. Compared to the 39 volumes of Washington's writings and the 50 to 60 volumes which will comprise the new edition now being published of Jefferson's, Henry's writings even today fill but one volume.

Though he became a legendary hero before his death in 1799, no one is more responsible for his popular image than William Wirt, who surmounted the problem of meager source materials by relying on recollections by Henry's surviving contemporaries and on his own imagination and rhetorical flourishes. What Parson Weems did for Washington in his cherry-tree extravaganza, Wirt did for Henry in his biography of 1817. A floridly romantic orator, a busy and able Virginia lawyer, a charming man with a minor reputation as a literary essayist, Wirt was far superior to the ineffable Parson, who shamelessly blended fiction with fact to promote morality and patriotism. Yet he was influenced by Weems' technique and amazing success, as well as by the curious historical standards of that day. He, too, made a major contribution to American mythology. Much of the subsequent writing on Henry has been a process of "de-Wirting" his over-blown hero. In history seminars scholars have long asked "Did Patrick Henry say this or did William Wirt?" and "Is it fact or is it Wirt?"

Yet his difficulties inspire sympathy, even though one is amazed that Wirt could do so much with so little. Unlike

Parson Weems, he painstakingly for over a decade collected
information, finding little but anecdotes and reminiscences. So indifferent were Virginians to preserving public
and private records of their great men that, as St. George
Tucker wrote Wirt, "Socrates himself would pass un-
noticed and forgotten in Virginia." Further, very little had
then been published on the American Revolution, and
that little was very poor. Strangely enough, what was in
Wirt's day considered the best history of it was by the
Italian, Charles W. Botta, who wrote his account originally
in Italian and in the classical tradition invented the
speeches there declaimed with Latin fervor by America's
Founding Fathers.

Scholars, understandably, are troubled by the way Wirt
brought into print Henry's classic Liberty or Death speech,
of which like his other Revolutionary orations there is no
contemporary text. But those who condemn Wirt for in-
venting this main prop of Henry's legendary fame always
overlook how popular Botta's "history" then was and how
Wirt, though tempted to emulate the inventive Italian,
rejected the idea of creating the text out of whole cloth as
"making too free with the sanctity of history." Nevertheless, he proceeded to reconstruct it from recollections of
men who some forty years before in Richmond's Saint
John's Church had heard Henry give it. Out of such raw
materials the author-orator worked up the famous oration.
To the pertinent question, "How much of it is Henry and
how much is Wirt?" the historian-detective must answer
that it is impossible to determine. Not surprisingly, it is
more concise and polished than extemporaneous speeches
later recorded. Yet its outline of argument and some of its
expressions are probably Henry's, since they seemed to
have burned themselves into men's memories. Certainly
its spirit is that of the fiery orator who in 1775 so power-

fully influenced Virginians and events leading to American independence.

His rebellious Parson's Cause speech of 1763, which first brought him fame as a lawyer of 27, Wirt did not attempt to reconstruct, but presented it in melodramatic descriptive passages. And he so treated the Treason speech of 1765 against the British-enacted Stamp Act, though here he did directly quote, from reminiscences, Henry's well-known words threatening George the Third with the tyrant's fate of Caesar and Charles the First, which incited the cry of treason, and his reply "If *this* be treason, make the most of it." Long criticized as most dubious, Wirt's account has been substantiated in our day by the discovery of many contemporary letters and the journal of a Frenchman who in Williamsburg heard and recorded the incident. This journal, alone, has Henry saying after he was called to order that he would beg pardon if in defending his country's dying liberty he had affronted the King, to whom he affirmed his loyalty. Many quibblers contend that this gesture of respect takes the fire out of his speech. Actually it was conventional down to 1776, even after a year of bloody fighting, to damn Parliament and affirm loyalty to "His Most Gracious Majesty"—but decidedly unconventional to threaten him with the fate of the decapitated Charles the First. Not only does the Frenchman confirm Wirt's account but he made later entries in his journal on the intense excitement caused by young Henry's bold defiance of British authority.

Even more vexatious a problem than the speeches, and peculiarly relevant to "the sanctity of history," was just how to portray Henry himself. Wirt's materials on him were so conflicting, "so recent and warm the prejudices of his friends and his adversaries," as he said, "that I had almost brought my mind to lay aside the project as one too tick-

lish for faithful execution." When he began it in 1805 he
assured Jefferson that Henry's "faults as well as his virtues
will be instructive, and I propose to myself to be his
biographer, not his panegyrist." But this high resolve by
good-hearted, sentimental William Wirt steadily weakened
as he became more upset by "some ugly traits in Henry's
character," as well as by lack of information on his career
which left "some pretty nearly as ugly blanks." Finally he
made his decision. He would fill in the blanks with "all
the plaster of Paris" at his command. And as to Henry
himself he would hold up to young men "the brighter side
of his character, only, to imitation." He would make his
Patrick Henry a "good text for a discourse on rhetoric,
patriotism and morals."

Dedicated to "The Young Men of Virginia" and written
with all of his extravagant romanticism, Wirt's biography
of 1817 portrayed Henry as a "giant genius" of unalloyed
virtues and unparalleled achievements, who symbolized
America's aspirations for freedom and her frontier democracy. Exaggerating always for dramatic effect, Wirt made
colonial Virginia's glories most glorious and the man who
became its leader a backwoods "plebeian," who forced the
scepter from the hand of King George and humbled the
proud Tidewater aristocracy. The plain people admired
him as a demigod, for, said Wirt, he was ever "as a sturdy
and wide spreading oak, beneath whose cool and refreshing
shade they might take refuge from those beams of aristocracy, that had played upon them so long, and with rather
an unpleasant heat." Such a paragon he explained only in
terms of a "Nature-taught genius," untouched by the hand
of art, to whom Nature herself had given a "Shakespeare's
genius and bade him . . . depend on that alone."

In portraying him as "the Homer of orators" Wirt really
applied all his "plaster of Paris." In the Treason speech,
for example, though Henry's obstacles were greater than

those of Hannibal crossing the Alps, with an eloquence as torrential as Niagara Falls, "in a voice of thunder and with the look of a god," he defied the King and crushed "the aristocracy . . . with as much ease as the unshorn Samson did the bands of the Philistines. He seized the pillars of the temple, shook them terribly, and seemed to threaten his opponents with ruin. It was an incessant storm of lightning and thunder, which struck them aghast. The fainthearted gathered courage . . . and cowards became heroes, while they gazed upon his exploits."

Such rhetorical exploits filled the life of Patrick Henry, as Wirt related it. Throughout his splendid career he had always "exhibited the impetuous charge of the gallant Francis the First" combined with "all the firm and dauntless constancy of Charles the Fifth." And when he retired from politics, said Wirt in conclusion, "no man had ever passed through so long a life of public service with a reputation more perfectly unspotted."

To an extraordinary degree he had presented "the brighter side of his character, only." Discerning Northern critics objected to his glorification of both Henry and Revolutionary Virginia. In the South, John Taylor of Caroline dismissed his book as "a splendid novel," while John Randolph of Roanoke lamented that his old hero had been set forth in "a wretched piece of fustian." Most interesting of all was the reaction of Thomas Jefferson, who for a decade had contributed to Wirt his reminiscences of Henry. "You have certainly vigorously practiced the precept" of speaking only good of the dead, he wrote Wirt. It was clear to him that Wirt had decided to write panegyric rather than history. To others Jefferson was more critical: "It is a poor book, written in bad taste, and gives an imperfect idea of Patrick Henry."

Nevertheless, it was outstandingly a popular success. A hero-worshipping public grasped it to its bosom as a liter-

ary masterpiece, one which admirably served its need both
to gratify and to stimulate patriotism. It became, as Wirt
hoped, a treasured textbook "on rhetoric, patriotism and
morals." Forty-one years later when Crawford's statue of
Henry was unveiled, it was going into its 16th edition. The 25th appeared in 1871, and other editions
continued to come out down into our time, while subsequent biographies and countless sketches have always used
it as a sourcebook. Unquestionably, William Wirt had
placed Patrick Henry on a folk-hero's pedestal, and in an
impressively enduring manner.

The popular image thus created with "all the plaster of
Paris" at Wirt's command has apparently remained unaf-
fected by the scholarly warfare which has long been waged
over "The Forest-born Demosthenes." Though the public
is unaware of it, attacks upon Wirt's "bright" image led
to counter-attacks, criticism to counter-criticism, and there
soon developed an enduring anti-Henry "dark" image. A
villain, to those of the Wirtian faction, had appeared in
this case of Patrick Henry, and to them that villain was
none other than Thomas Jefferson.

Strangely enough, Jefferson contributed greatly to both
Bright and Dark images, for in this story he plays a commendatory and a derogatory role. Wirt's "perfectly unspotted" hero he in general praised highly but in detailed
dispraise noted many very "ugly spots." This has caused
Jefferson to be regarded as the most generous of political
foes and as a character-assassin who continued to blacken
Henry's image long after his death in 1799. His more
objective admirers find his conduct puzzling. Though
usually glossed over by his biographers, Jefferson was often
warmly and sweepingly partisan, as ardent friends on
occasion admitted: "his fault is, that he is too unguarded,"
noted Wirt in 1809; he had, as James Madison once said,
"a habit . . . of expressing in strong and round terms,

impressions of the moment." Yet after partisan battles
ceased he usually adhered to that code Henry always followed and which he himself well expressed as to his one-
time rival John Adams, that honest men need not detest
one another or dis-socialize because they differ in politics.
His treatment of Henry, his one-time leader, seems out of
character. It sharply contrasts with that of Judge John
Tyler, who also came to differ with Henry, yet retained
for him always the warmest admiration. In short, Jefferson's perplexing conduct is a sort of riddle within the
enigma which is Patrick Henry.

Wirt was aware of his bias, and of his faults of memory,
when in his preface he thanked Jefferson, Judge Tyler,
and others for their reminiscences but said they were
sometimes "so diametrically opposed to each other" as to
force him to depart from their views. How greatly he
departed from Jefferson's is revealed by nine manuscript
letters from 1805 to 1816 which Jefferson wrote him,
recently acquired by the University of Virginia Library.
His high praise of Henry in them Wirt readily printed.
But his many "ugly" things he omitted entirely, or, if he
mentioned any of them at all it was to refute or to soften
them down in innocuousness.

In the first of these letters, of August 4, 1805, which
must suffice as a sample, Jefferson paid tribute to Henry
as the chief leader of the Revolution in Virginia, with
whom "down to the year 1781" he had been most cordially
intimate and acted "in perfect concert." Henry was "the
greatest orator that ever lived"—though on other occasions
Jefferson, no orator himself, would remark that after a
thrilling speech he would sometimes ask himself: "What
the devil did he say?" He was also "the best humored man
in society I almost ever knew." Further, "he had a consummate knowledge of the human heart" which, with "his
eloquence, enabled him to attain a degree of popularity

with the people at large never perhaps equalled." And yet
Jefferson's criticism was as harsh as his praise was high.
For in this same letter, and even more so in later ones, he
disparaged Henry's intellectual qualities, said his legal
knowledge "was not worth a copper," and bluntly declared
that he was "avaritious and rotten hearted. His two great
passions were love of money and of fame," with love of
money always predominating.

Of key significance here is his reference to the year 1781.
For it was then that Henry had supported an inquiry into
Jefferson's conduct as war governor during the British
invasion of Virginia; and Jefferson, in anguish at being
the target of intense criticism, had bitterly turned on his
political tutor and chieftain. Privately he then said Henry
was "all tongue, without either head or heart." And he
readily believed hearsay rumors, now regarded by scholars
as unfounded, that Henry at this crisis plotted to make
himself a military dictator with absolute powers. It was
not a public break, but from 1781 on in letters to friends
he expressed his distrust and dislike of Henry, his politics
and character. And when Henry in 1799, on the eve of his
death, joined Washington and his Federalists against Jefferson and his Republicans, he became thenceforth, to
Thomas Jefferson at least, The Great Apostate.

It was this criticism, expressed privately to Wirt and to
others, when later it was in part published that set off the
battle over Henry's reputation. From that time to this
Jefferson's Dark image of him has been reflected, and often
exaggerated, in historical studies and especially in biographies of Jefferson, Madison, and other political opponents. Because of it many an account of Henry has become
an anti-Jefferson tract, for his defenders have spent much
more time "de-Jeffersonizing" than "de-Wirting" Patrick
Henry.

One of the first guns fired in his defense was by his

grandson, William Wirt Henry, in 1867. Three years later that free-wheeling iconoclast, Edward A. Pollard, ridiculed "the mess of inconsistencies" in both Dark and Bright images. He attacked Wirt for idolizing Henry and condemned Jefferson for his thinly-disguised "almost fierce envy or contempt" of him, and his "manifestly false" and cruel description of Henry as an ignorant, uncouth fellow who preferred the low company of overseers and changed his shirt but once a fortnight. In 1887 Moses Coit Tyler, in a biography far superior to Wirt's, defended Henry against all who had scoffed at his mental prowess and social graces, diminished his oratorical and legal fame, and blackened his character by calling him a detestable demagogue and political apostate. In 1891 Henry's grandson re-entered the fray with three glowingly commemorative volumes. He was followed in this century by several popular biographies in the Wirtian tradition and, in 1957, by Robert D. Meade's outstanding volume on Henry's early life down through 1774. Though Meade has unearthed no new mass of letters, and his eighty pages of footnotes attest not only diligent research but the perplexing problems he faced, his scholarly portrait has done much to reveal the youthful Henry more clearly as a man rather than a myth.

But the battle over Bright and Dark images still goes on. Some historians contend that the portrait Meade is painting is too sympathetic, too Wirtian. It is brighter than that in such recent scholarly works as John R. Alden's history of the South in the Revolution or David Mays' Edmund Pendleton, Henry's lifelong conservative rival. Dumas Malone's Jefferson reflects his hero's dark views, and black indeed is Henry's portrait as a demagogue in Irving Brant's Madison. Scholars and especially biographers, always humanly fallible, will always have their conflicting interpretations of public men. But this is particularly true

of Patrick Henry, about whom many questions are still
asked, many riddles remain to be solved.

Acutely aware of this and of his own fallibility, the
historian-detective ventures to make his summary report
on what this elusive man really was like. He is encouraged
to do so by the recent scholarship, impressive in range and
quality, on the men and events of Henry's Revolutionary
Epoch. For this has dispelled a good deal of the fog long
obscuring him, which caused Pollard to cry out: "Is the
'Forest-born Demosthenes,' after all, a mythical personage?"

The flesh-and-blood man who is now emerging was
neither Wirt's "Nature-taught genius," a classical scholar
lolling at pastoral ease rapturously reading Livy in Latin,
nor Jefferson's ignorant abhorrer of all books, who would
not even read in English the agreeable prose of David
Hume. We now know that he was tutored by an unusually
well-educated father, the product of the University of
Aberdeen, and his formal education was very much better
than Washington's. Yet as with Washington, when compared to Jefferson his intellectual limitations in depth and
range are obvious, his cultural interests insignificant.
Socially, he rivalled neither of these two wealthy men,
being more typical of the usual Virginia planter whose
way of life was modest compared to that of the Squire of
Mount Vernon and the Master of Monticello. He was not
the traditional Huck Finn ne'er-do-well or Davy Crockett
"plebeian." Rather he was an ambitious, hard-working,
though very amiable and popular member of a reputable
family and of a substantial middle class gentry.

After failing as farmer and storekeeper, his driving ambi-
tion, persuasive personality, and superb oratorical gifts
brought him success in law and politics. As a legislative
leader, he was "omnipotent" for a generation in an era of
personal rather than party politics. His genius lay in boldly
proposing and eloquently debating measures general in

nature, while his bland indifference to laborious detail irked his devoted followers. As a lawyer, he was inferior to Jefferson in legal knowledge yet as a resourceful practitioner he made many a "copper" in the fees he commanded in the high courts even in civil cases. In criminal cases and in the county courts he was the unrivalled "monarch of the bar." His mastery of jurors, witnesses, and opposing counsel gave rise to many amusing stories of his wit and ingenuity, for he utilized all the devices of the trial lawyer, all the skills which the great orator has in common with the great actor.

As lawyer and political leader he brought into play what Jefferson called his "consummate knowledge of the human heart." And this the historian-detective would emphasize as a mainspring of his fame. For "the great Patrick" had an unequalled knack of understanding and winning the trust of people. With "the lower and middling classes" especially he was on familiar terms, having to a marked degree "the common touch"—a precious thing in any public man, and one lacking in the stately Washington and foreign to the scholarly Jefferson. Their national fame came to surpass that of "The Trumpet of the Revolution," whose war and postwar activities were confined to Virginia. But in Virginia, in her golden age of great men, no man's fame in politics exceeded Henry's. This fact is usually obscured by the excesses of both idolaters and iconoclasts. Yet Jefferson, in his commendatory role, only voiced general opinion when he wrote Wirt that Henry's popularity was "never perhaps equalled" and, as he later wrote, that down to 1799 Patrick Henry "through a long and active life had been the idol of his country beyond any man who ever lived."

But did he make proper use of this public trust and of his great talents? Or did he betray and debase them—as charged by those who write him down as a self-seeking

demagogue, expanding remarks made by Jefferson in his
derogatory role, as in 1799 after Henry came out against
him when Jefferson said he feared the man's "intriguing
and cajoling talents, for which he is still more remarkable
than for his eloquence," or as in 1805 when he wrote Wirt
that Henry was "avaritious and rotten hearted," dominated by his "love of money and of fame."

Actually he loved fame no more than Jefferson, even less
perhaps, since he declined successive offers of the highest
national posts from Presidents Washington and Adams.
And his unrivalled fame in Virginia was not restricted to
"the lower and middling classes." It extended to "gentlemen of long-tailed families," who placed a premium on
oratory but decidedly did not relish demagoguery. To
write him down as a rabble-rouser is, indeed, to indict the
Virginia of the golden age with its high standards of honor
and integrity; a Virginia in which it was very rare for the
class issue of poor against rich ever to be raised. It is to
indict the freeholders who unfailingly elected Henry their
representative, the county oligarchies of substantial plant-
ers who controlled local politics, and the highly respectable
gentlemen who made Henry their leader in the colonial
House of Burgesses and later in the General Assembly. It
is inconceivable that such a demagogue in those days of
1776 that tried men's souls could be elected the first governor of an independent Virginia—elected not by the people
but by their leaders in the Assembly. It is incredible that
these leaders of the Great Generation of Virginians, in the
critical war and postwar years, could choose as their leader
such a base creature and elect him not once but six times
governor of the proud Old Dominion.

Such facts apply with equal force to the charge, similarly
exaggerated by partisan writers, that Henry was dominated
by his "avaritious" love of money. As a renowned lawyer,
much in demand, he was able to charge higher fees than

his colleagues; or, as Jefferson expressed it to Wirt, from "poor devils" in criminal cases "it was always understood that he squeezed exorbitant fees." Like Jefferson and other Virginians, most notably Washington, Henry invested—or "speculated"—in frontier lands. He did so on a large scale in later life when, debt-ridden after years in public service, he sought by such means to augment his income from a revived law practice. He has been criticized for these land transactions, but in them his conduct while sharp and shrewd was honest. Critical as Jefferson was as to Henry's "avarice," the scholarly editor of the new definitive edition of his writings, Julian P. Boyd, states that there is no evidence that he ever considered him to be venal or corrupt. In his last years Henry was determined not to die in debt and poverty—as Jefferson later did in such a pathetic, heart-wrenching manner. Priding himself on being a good businessman, he was determined to provide for his children—all seventeen of them. As a devoted father of a household where the cradle never ceased to rock, as a self-made man relatively unaided as were Jefferson and Washington by wealth from inheritance or marriage, Patrick Henry had reasons enough to be concerned with money matters.

Yet his was always a gay spirit, and Virginians frequently said that the fieriest of orators was the "best humored" of men. In his youth they noted his "passion for music, dancing, and pleasantry." In his maturity they noted that this fiddle-playing, story-telling, yet increasingly religious man, plain of dress, "conciliating and abounding in good humor," was always most courteous to his opponents. Surprisingly free from the feuding and bitter recriminations of so many public men, he was outstanding in crediting his rivals with honesty if not with good judgment. His sharpest remark of Madison was that he was more bookworm political theorist than realistic leader of men. And his harshest criticism of Jefferson was about his preference for French chefs and high-toned French cooking. In that downright, earthy manner which endeared him to the people of Virginia, Henry observed that the Master of Monticello by disdaining honest fatback and turnip greens had "abjured his native vittles."

While "moderate and mild, and in religious matters a Saint," as a Virginian said of him in 1774, he was "the very Devil in politics" and in his oratory a veritable "Son of Thunder." Scholars may dispute about Henry as Devil and as Saint, and about the text of early orations. But as the Son of Thunder he deserves his fame as "The Trumpet of the Revolution." In 1765 on his first days in the House of Burgesses, with his Stamp Act resolves backed by his Treason speech, he spectacularly seized control from the conservative Tidewater oligarchy and powerfully stiffened resistance throughout British America. Thereafter by his bold leadership, which won the support of Jefferson and Washington, and by his magnificent eloquence he continued to give a decisive impulse to Revolutionary events. And he did this, notably, by his demand in March of 1775, made effective by his soul-stirring Liberty or Death speech, for arming Virginia for a war he said was inevitable and which "we must fight!"

Two months later he himself led his armed neighbors against the royal governor in Virginia's "first overt act of the war." However, it was clear that his talents were not those of a Washington, and his career as commander of her armed forces was short. Yet he was always more than a great orator. Often overlooked is his vital work in organizing resistance in Virginia and in fostering a common American front, as when he so vividly declared in the Continental Congress of 1774: "I am not a Virginian, but an American." Or the decisively democratic impulse he gave events in 1776 when he aided George Mason in framing Virginia's first constitution which proclaimed the inalienable rights of all men and asserted Virginia's independence a month before Jefferson's Declaration asserted it for all America. As an able war governor for three successive terms from 1776 to 1779 he had George Rogers Clark conquer the Northwest and he supported General Washington and his Continentals in such a stout-hearted way as to win Washington's lasting gratitude.

All this gives point to George Mason's remark that Patrick Henry's overpowering eloquence was but "the smallest part of his merit. He is, in my opinion, the first man upon this continent, as well in abilities as public virtues." And it brings to mind the handsome tribute paid Henry years later by John Adams, usually so sharply critical of his contemporaries, who had served with him in the Continental Congress of 1774 and 1775. To Adams, also, he was far more than "the Demosthenes of the age," being a man "of deep reflection, keen sagacity, clear foresight, daring enterprise, inflexible intrepidity, and untainted integrity, with an ardent zeal for the liberties, the honor, and felicity of his country and his species."

His role in Virginia politics has been most confusingly portrayed. Though he had no clear-cut program of domestic reforms, traditionally he has been over-simplified as Wirt's buckskin radical who fought the cause of backwoods democracy against Tidewater aristocracy. Some scholars now doubt that he had any such cause to fight. In this they go too far, for the sectional conflict was always a factor, even though it has been long overstressed. Actually politics then were complex and fluid. Parties had yet to emerge, all were whigs and after 1776 all republicans, and the line between liberal and conservative often blurred, since men constantly shifted as issues arose, differing often only as to means and timing. An unawareness of this has resulted in charges of inconsistency, against Henry and

others as well, with some writers over-simplifying Henry
not only as a flaming radical but as a diehard conservative.
On the whole, no man better appraised or led public
opinion; no man had a better sense of timing. Yet it is not
true, as said by Jefferson and by partisan writers who still
echo him, that Henry was always with and never against
the tide; that he was always in the van of an already formed
public opinion. This is contradicted by his boldness against
Britain and by such unpopular acts as insisting after the
war on the return of the detested Tories, attempting to
solve racial conflicts by state bounties to whites who would
marry Indians, or defending Baptist preachers imprisoned
in their fight for religious freedom. On balance, his record
is that of a liberal. But as such he was out-rivalled by Jefferson who, when Henry was war governor, championed
a legislative program of far-reaching democratic social reforms.

Even so, Henry, as always, remained the dominating
leader, and a most independent one. Once when he
frowned on one of Jefferson's reform measures as impracti-
cable, the exasperated Master of Monticello wrote Madison that for the measure's eventual success all they could
do was to hope and pray for Henry's death. On another
occasion his democratic policies had so offended such conservatives as Landon Carter, that Carter believing a false
report of Henry's death rejoiced exceedingly. The historian-
detective is greatly impressed by the man's tremendous
power, his persuasive talents, his unequalled popularity.
Again and again he finds Jefferson, Madison, Washington,
and others asking just how Henry stood on such and such
an issue—and just how he stood often if not always meant
its success or failure.

But he failed, failed magnificently and by a hair's
breadth, to prevent Virginia in 1788 from ratifying the
Constitution. He wanted a more effective Union govern-

ment, but he then opposed the new government desired by Washington and championed by Madison as one that would consolidate all power in itself, and be dominated by the Northeast to the detriment of the South and West. Like Jefferson, he was much concerned by the Constitution's lack of a Bill of Rights. By demanding amendments protecting the basic civil liberties of individuals he made a constructive contribution. On eighteen of the Virginia Convention's twenty-three days the Son of Thunder battled Madison's formidable nationalists. His speeches alone, some the ablest of his career, amounted to one-fourth of all those recorded. In his last great effort as he warned of dire perils ahead Nature herself joined her "Nature-taught orator" by a storm which darkened the chamber and flashed bolts of lightning amid crashes of thunder; the combination was such that the final vote was put off until the next day.

In the best democratic tradition he accepted the majority decision and pledged allegiance to the new government. But he still dominated the Virginia Assembly. There, as Washington reported, Patrick Henry "has only to say, let this be law, and it is law." He excluded Madison from the Senate, gerrymandered the state, and saw to it that the men sent to Congress would fight for the Bill of Rights he insistently demanded. Just before "the great Patrick" at the height of his popularity and power retired from politics in 1790 he had Virginia sharply protest Alexander Hamilton's assumption of the state debts, a Federalist policy enacted into law only with the help of Hamilton's colleague, Secretary of State Jefferson. In his states rights views of 1788 and 1790 Henry set a pattern for the Republican party which slowly began to emerge—a party, ironically enough, led at first by his nationalistic opponent in 1788, James Madison, and then by Thomas Jefferson.

The ironies of history are well illustrated in Henry's

last years. His brief reappearance in public life in 1799, on the eve of his death, to combat the states rights Virginia and Kentucky Resolutions of Madison and Jefferson, was as dramatic as his entrance in 1765 and far more controversial. Was this the noblest act of his career, as the Washingtonians said? Or was it the ignoble act of The Great Apostate, as the Jeffersonians said?

Only by getting above the intense partisanship of that day, and its reflection in much historical writing, can one fairly judge Henry—and Madison, Jefferson, or Pendleton. As issues changed and parties emerged, all these men had shifted positions. The partisan labels then applied to Washingtonian Federalists, "monarchical, aristocratical, pro-British," seem especially incongruous applied by the Master of Monticello to homespun Patrick Henry, "Trumpet of the Revolution." His charge of political apostasy, which he also made against Washington, Henry might well have indignantly flung back at Jefferson, and even more so at Madison, Pendleton, and the vast majority of his opponents in 1788 who by 1799 had become states rights "radical, anarchic, pro-French" Jeffersonian Republicans. This he did not do. Adhering to his code that honest men may honestly differ, he merely said that he was loyal to his lifelong democratic principles and the Constitutional Union to which he had pledged himself in 1788.

During these last years he rigorously held himself aloof from all politics, state and national. Working hard at law cases and land transactions, he paid off his debts, provided for his many children, and when he retired from all business in 1794 had a small fortune. Part of this came from the raising of his state securities to par value by Hamilton's assumption of state debts in 1790. This financial windfall was the sole reason given by Jefferson and by later detractors to explain why Henry aligned himself with Washington in 1799. As Irving Brant in his *James Madison* puts it, because of the money so made Henry deserted his principles of 1788 and "was attached to the Union by the best Hamiltonian cement."

This is much too simple an explanation and does Henry gross injustice. If he had become a Federalist during these money-making years why should Jefferson as well as Washington have tried so hard to woo him out of his retirement into their respective parties? And woo him they did, so great was the prestige of "the old Governor," so magic still the name of Patrick Henry. On the ground of ill health he refused to become Chief Justice or Washington's Secretary of State or Minister to Spain or John Adams' Minister to France. He turned down a Senatorship from Virginia and a sixth term as governor when elected in 1796 by the same Republicans who that year voted to elect Jefferson president. And of no avail were Jefferson's efforts in 1792 and again in 1795, when through a mutual friend he tried to satisfy Henry "that there is no remain of disagreeable sentiment towards him on my part. I was once sincerely affectionated towards him and it accords with my philosophy to encourage the tranquillizing passions."

It was Washington, not Jefferson, who at last wooed him out of his retirement. From Mount Vernon early in 1799 came such an urgent call to battle that Henry could not resist. Washington was insistent that the great crisis—one threatening the Union and pregnant with "the horrors of anarchy" which Henry wrote him in 1795 could alone get him back into politics—had definitely arrived. Henry must once again exert his old leadership. He must stand for election to the Assembly and there combat Madison and his Virginia Resolutions, which not only denied the constitutionality of the Federal Alien and Sedition laws but had stirred up such a popular frenzy and turmoil as to endanger the very foundations of the republic.

Whether one accepts the Washington-Henry view of the

crisis of 1799, or the contrary Jefferson-Madison view that
what really was at issue were basic civil rights, the historian-detective is forced to pay tribute to Patrick Henry's
gallantry, courage, and patriotism. He was then in very
poor health, an enfeebled prematurely old man, desiring
only the tranquility of his modest home at Red Hill. His
decision publicly to join forces with Washington, and
others of the weak Federalist minority such as John Marshall and Light-Horse Harry Lee, was a most unpopular
one in a Virginia overwhelmingly Jeffersonian. In fairness
to Henry and to "the sanctity of history" one must emphasize that it was decidedly not the decision of a self-seeking
demagogue dominated by an "avaritious" love of money
and of cheaply earned fame.

Since 1790 when he had "bid adieu" to politics, his
nonpartisan views on the issues of those tumultuous years,
privately expressed, had moved him closer to Washington's
position. As a man "moderate and mild, and in religious
matters a Saint," he abhorred the atheism and bloody
excesses of Revolutionary France, an arrogant and ra-
pacious France waging in 1799 an undeclared war on his
country which had forced Washington out of his retirement to become once again America's commander-in-chief.
As a realistic politician, he correctly predicted that "the
horrors of anarchy" in the French republic would lead to
the despotism of a Bonaparte; and he feared a like fate for
his own republic. By 1799 he had come to a matured con-
viction that the policies of a Washington and not a Jefferson would best guarantee orderly liberty and an enduring
American Union. To the battle call from Mount Vernon
he responded as he had assured Washington he would,
since "I should be unworthy the character of a republican
or an honest man if I withheld from the government my
best and most zealous efforts because in its adoption I
opposed it in its unamended form."

And so it was that the feeble old man dramatically re-appeared in March of 1799, defying the powerful Jeffersonians who feared and reviled him, thrilling the people as of old with his magic eloquence, and providing them with fresh anecdotes to swell the Patrick Henry saga. He won their votes, as always. But this last desperate effort was too taxing. It forced the gallant warrior to his bed, and to his death, three months after his final victory.

His simple tombstone slab at Red Hill has but these words: "His fame his best epitaph." His popular fame as "The Trumpet of the Revolution" is justly an enduring one. Most Americans who gaze at that slab at Red Hill, or at the Richmond statue unveiled a century ago, are unconcerned with scholarly efforts to paint his portrait more fully, with both the lights and the shades of reality. It suffices that he continues to be, as he was in his own day, the unequalled and ever-inspiring orator of liberty. And it is pleasing to note that this Bright image of him Jefferson came more to see as the years mellowed his partisan views and, nearing his own death, he harked back ever more to those stirring days when he had been "sincerely affectionated towards him." Not only was his eloquence "sublime" but as "our leader," said the Master of Monticello to Daniel Webster in 1824, "he was far above all . . . in the Revolution." Indeed, "it is not now easy to say what we should have done without Patrick Henry."

LECTURE

TWO

Washington: "Freedom's Myth" and "More Than Man"

WHEN TO "CANNON'S DEAFENING ROAR AND JOYOUS THROB of drum" Crawford's equestrian statue of General George Washington, with its standing figures of Patrick Henry and Thomas Jefferson, was unveiled on February 22, 1858, amid whirling snowflakes in Richmond's Capitol Square, orators and poets for two days vied with one another in extolling The Father of His Country as a hero unequalled in all history. Celebrating in verse these "mystic rites" of patriotism, James Barron Hope deified Washington as America's "Messiah" and John R. Thompson pronounced Capitol Square "henceforth to all a consecrated place that holds a sacred shrine." At the mere mention of The Patriot Father's "magic name," declared Governor Henry A. Wise, "Civil Discord hushes into awed silence, schisms and sections are subdued and vanish; for, in the very naming of that name, there is . . . the spell of Order, and Liberty, and Law, and the strength and beauty of *National Union*." Edward Everett of Massachusetts in the most famous of Washington orations, one which from 1856 to 1860 he repeated 129 times, also emphasized the father-image to

soften sectional asperities then driving North and South
apart. But the fiery secessionist from Alabama, William
Lowndes Yancey, stressed Washington not as the symbol
of Union but of Rebellion; of a people's inalienable right
to overthrow an unjust government, so eloquently proclaimed by Henry's tongue and Jefferson's pen, so incom-
parably vindicated by Washington's Revolutionary sword.

These ceremonies of a century ago are interesting to the
historian-detective and to all who would separate Washington the man from Washington the myth. They reveal that
the myth even then was a formidable one. They point up
the problem which still besets the historian—how can he
portray the man when he has been so long obscured by an
almost impenetrable *mystique* of excessive veneration? At
Richmond in 1858 this obscuring legend was presented in
all its many aspects. Pictured there was not a flesh-and-
blood man but a godlike abstraction, as devoid of life as
Thomas Crawford's bronze statue. And in his various
symbols the folk-hero was then as always employed by men
to advance their own aspirations. More truly than he
realized did the Virginia poet of that day acclaim Washington in these words:

> And future ages, when thy fame they scan,
> Will deem thee Freedom's myth—thou more than man.

How explain this transfiguration of a mortal Virginian
into an immortal Olympian—into "Freedom's myth" and
"more than man"?

Like all folk-heroes he was a blurred figure, blended of
fact and wishful fancy. Those who in the various media
of art presented his image selected and excluded to suit
their purpose, emphasizing aspects which they and the
people believed or were eager to believe. Their hero-worship was both an expression of patriotism and a stimulus
to it. People always tend to over-idealize their leaders, but

the need for heroic symbols was especially acute during the critical Revolutionary Epoch. Americans then rejected the ritual of monarchy, with its father-image of King George. Out of their need and their pride they created a new republican ritual, a secular religion of "mystic rites" which still flourishes with such symbols as The Flag and patriotic relics and shrines. Since individuals most effectively symbolize emotions and ideals, Washington with his commanding merits understandably came to personify qualities upon which people placed the highest value. He became the Father-Hero of America's Creative Age, "first in war and first in peace," who held together a Union of diverse regions. He led his people to victory, rejected a military dictatorship, and became the champion of government by laws and not by men. Exalted into a demigod, Americans proudly acclaimed him as the product and the symbol of their republic's greatness.

This apotheosis began in his lifetime. It survived contemporary criticism of him as General and as President. It was greatly accelerated at his death in December of 1799 by the many eulogies, of which over 300 were published of the many more delivered. Prototypes of all later orations, they so extravagantly praised him that Mrs. John Adams at the time discerningly remarked, "Simple truth is his best, his greatest eulogy." Alas, simple truth was long to be disregarded. And by none so flagrantly as the Reverend Mason Locke Weems of Dumfries, Virginia. His biography, appearing shortly after the hero's death, and in many subsequent editions, did most to establish Washington's enduring popular image. As an influential myth-maker the extraordinary Parson Weems deserves some attention.

A jolly, roguish Episcopal minister turned author and book peddler, Weems travelled the country in his Jersey wagon, selling his own and other books after first attracting a crowd by playing his fiddle or preaching a sensational sermon. His main purpose in life, he once said, was "to *Enlighten*, to *dulcify*, and Exalt Human Nature—by GOOD BOOKS." He keenly understood the average American, who relished as most readable and instructive the Parson's moralistic and patriotic writings. In his best-selling tracts he fought against gaming, drinking, and duelling. He urged early marriages and large families in his famous *Matrimonial Tattoo Against Bachelors,* later issued under the revealing title of *Hymen's Recruiting-Sergeant; or, the Maid's and Bachelor's Friend, Containing a Very Seasonable and Savoury Dissertation on Love, Courtship, and Matrimony. With a Very Fine Flourish on True Beauty* [and] *Some Elegant Songs.* Whether he was advising the lovelorn, converting the sinner, or inspiring the patriot, everything he did was done with extraordinary gusto. He always made a fine flourish to the popular taste. Discovering the people's avid hunger for books on American heroes, he became the poor man's Plutarch. And in writing his biographies, whether of Franklin, Penn, or Francis Marion, the Parson had no qualms whatsoever about committing the scholar's sin of "making too free with the sanctity of history."

This was especially true of his Washington, which he had "very nearly primed and cocked . . . for the gaping millions," as he said, some months before his subject's death. Having collected anecdotes, created others, invented conversations and speeches, with an unrestrained imagination, an eye for the telling phrase, and a lyrical free-flowing style, he blended all into a very seasonable and savoury dissertation for the good of mankind and his own profit. "'Tis artfully drawn up, enlivened with anecdotes, and in my humble opinion marvellously fitted" for the American taste, he wrote his publisher in June of 1799. "What say you to printing it for me" with a frontispiece of "The Guardian Angel of his Country" with this inscription:

" 'Go thy way old George. Die when thou wilt, we shall never look upon thy like again.' " Emphasizing Washington's exemplary virtues, it would promote morality and patriotism, and for author and publisher make "a world of pence and popularity."

Published early in 1800 amid the eulogies on Washington's death, it was then and thenceforth an astounding success. Though scholarly critics even then damned it as "a literary antic" unworthy of its hero, in six years it went through nine printings and well into this century attained a total of 80 best-selling editions. Weems swelled each early edition with new and dubious anecdotes. "The Fifth edition, greatly improved," as he announced, was published in Augusta, Georgia, in 1806, with the revealing title of *The Life of Washington the Great. Enriched with a number of Very Curious Anecdotes, Perfectly in Character, and Equally Honorable to Himself, and Exemplary to his Young Countrymen.* It was this edition which first contained the cherry-tree story, the most famous of his many "very curious anecdotes." It well illustrates the Parson's inimitable style with all of its moralistic embellishments which both instructed and delighted generation after generation of hero-worshipping Americans:

When George was about six years old, he was made the wealthy master of a hatchet! Of which, like most little boys, he was immoderately fond, and was constantly going about chopping every thing that came in his way. One day, in the garden, where he often amused himself hacking his mother's pea-sticks, he unluckily tried the edge of his hatchet on the body of a beautiful young English cherry-tree, which he barked so terribly that I don't believe the tree ever got the better of it. The next morning the old gentleman finding out what had befallen his tree, which, by the by, was a great favourite, came into the house, and with much warmth asked for the mischievous author, declaring at the same time that he would not have taken five guineas for his tree. Nobody could tell him any thing about it. Presently George and his hatchet made their appearance. *George,* said his father, *do you know who killed that beautiful little cherry-tree yonder in the garden?* This was a *tough question;* and George staggered under it for a moment; but quickly recovering himself, and looking at his father, with the sweet face of youth brightened with the inexpressible charm of all conquering truth, he bravely cried out, *I can't tell a lie, Pa; you know I can't tell a lie. I did cut it with my hatchet. Run to my arms, you dearest boy,* cried his father in transports, *run to my arms; glad am I, George, that you killed my tree; for you have paid me for it a thousand fold. Such an act of heroism in my son is more worth than a thousand trees, though blossomed with silver, and their fruits of purest gold.*

It was a copybook hero that Weems presented. A flawless character fully developed in the child explained Washington's rise to phenomenal success, not only as General and President but as the young Colonel who won the rich widow Custis, at which the Parson exulted: "Here was a proper rise for you!" Anecdote followed anecdote to illustrate particular virtues. Some of them—such as George tattling on his schoolmates for fighting and he himself sometimes severely rebuking them—made him for modern taste a thorough prig. But the Parson enlightened and "dulcified" millions of Americans down through the years as he blithely proceeded to point the moral and adorn the tale of the proper little boy with the hatchet, carrying him through a fabulous career in which he freed his country from tyranny, guided it into the Promised Land, and as Saint George was finally wafted aloft to heaven on angels' wings:

Swift on angels' wings the brightening saint ascended; while voices more than human were warbling through the happy regions, and hymning the great procession towards the gates of heaven. His glorious coming was seen afar off; and myriads of mighty angels hastened forth, with golden harps, to welcome the honoured stranger.

Parson Weems, the Virginia hedge-priest, had most successfully canonized the Hero of Mount Vernon. For years thereafter treasured family copies of his biography vied with reproductions of Gilbert Stuart's idealized portrait as the most popular stimuli to patriotic devotion. As early as 1811 a Russian diplomat noted that every American believes "he owes his independence, happiness, and wealth" to this hero, and he "considers it his sacred duty to have a likeness of Washington in his home just as we [Russians have in our homes our icons or] images of God's saints." Not only was the Parson's textbook on patriotism and morality reproduced in many editions but it set the pattern for innumerable 19th century biographies, some of them very popular in their day, and for countless sketches and eulogies. All used his ministerial panegyric as a sourcebook, and all deified their subject. Only too typical was the best-selling contribution of Horatio Hastings Weld with its revealing opening line: "The first word of infancy should be Mother, the second Father, and the third WASHINGTON." But their demigod was never as lively a hero as the Parson's. This was especially true of the three major biographies, which reverently emphasized Washington's public life, and successfully congealed him into marble, a national deity august and austere.

Such was he in Chief Justice John Marshall's five-volume biography of 1804-1807, aptly described by John Adams as "a Mausoleum, 100 feet square at the base, and 200 feet high." More history than biography, with the hero not born until volume two, with large parts lifted without credit from other writers, with volume five so partisan that Jefferson called it libelous, in it Washington always in military or court dress with godlike tread stalks stiffly through the many, many, turgid pages. Yet it went into many editions, and for years was widely read. So was Jared Sparks' biography of 1837, the first volume of his twelve-volume edition of Washington's writings. Admittedly the worshipper of an impeccable hero, this Harvard historian blended Weems' priggishness with Marshall's glacier-like formality. As editor he prudishly altered or omitted expressions by Washington that he thought were vulgar. Equally concerned with protecting the hero from himself was Washington Irving, in his five-volume biography of the 1850s. Though he detected a smile on the General's face after the victory at Trenton, Irving, too, presented a coldly dignified and imposing demigod.

This same awe and veneration dulled the critical faculties of the major historians who wrote on the Revolutionary Epoch. George Bancroft, for example, saw clearly the Hand of God in American history and Washington as divinely ordained. So it was with John Fiske, though he preferred to write in terms of the Laws of History. With others they made him so dominating a figure as unjustly to dwarf his many military and civil colleagues. Their influence carried over into the twentieth century. It was conspicuously represented by Albert J. Beveridge, who in his classic biography of John Marshall fervidly declared: "Washington was the Government. Washington was the Revolution." And a few years later Beveridge's words were echoed by the thousand clarion tongues of the Washington Bicentennial of 1932.

The traditional image of "Freedom's myth" was presented by the Bicentennial Commission in every medium then known to Madison Avenue hucksters and side-show barkers, among whom its director, Congressman Sol Bloom, was once pre-eminent. There were Bicentennial stamps, coins, medals, pageants, home-study courses, and even books in Braille. "Placed in each school room of every school in the United States," proudly said Mr. Bloom, was a copy of Stuart's idealized portrait "reproduced in ten colors." There was a special Bicentennial song by "Yankee Doodle Dandy" George M. Cohan, a special march by "March King" John Philip Sousa, a special poem by "Man with the Hoe" Edwin Markham, who hymned Washington as a hero who "toiled with men until he flamed with God." A special corps of historians headed by Albert Bushnell Hart of Harvard often scaled the familiar heights of idolatry. For example, Samuel C. Vestal concluded his study of Washington as General in words Parson Weems might well have envied: "He was bolder than Alexander, more crafty than Hannibal, wiser than Caesar, more prudent than Gustavus Adolphus, more resourceful than Frederick, more sagacious than Napoleon, and more successful than Scipio; and his star will not pale by the side of theirs."

Thus into our own time has this blending of fiction with fact, of mythology with history, obscured the man's real qualities which, as Abigail Adams long ago said, simple truth alone could reveal. A paragon of moral perfection, he was unblemished by human frailties or human passions. Daniel Webster earlier spoke for all eulogists when he asked, rhetorically and unnecessarily, "What virtue was wanting in him, or what vice was ever laid to his charge?" Men long ago became dissatisfied merely to extol him above all other heroes sacred and profane. The apotheosis was complete when they compared Washington to Christ and his mother to the Virgin Mary—to be echoed today by those in Fredericksburg, Virginia, who attract patriotic pilgrims with signs reading "This Way to the Home of Mary the Mother of Washington."

Pious pilgrims to such patriotic shrines are not shocked by what scholars may deem sacrilegious. But they would be shocked by the question Nathaniel Hawthorne once asked: "Did anybody ever see Washington nude? It is inconceivable," he answered, for it seems that "he was born with his clothes on, and his hair powdered, and made

a stately bow on his first appearance in the world." Shock-
ing also would be some of the minor themes that have
questioned the long-dominant demigod theme. For the
myth has excluded or blurred many things to suit its
purpose. It has dealt harshly with those who would present
him with simple truth, and thus save him from a fate
worse than deification—the fate of a hero so glorified as to
become, to intelligent admirers, more boring than inspiring. For as Emerson once warned the Washington myth-
makers, "every hero becomes a bore at last."

Excluded by the myth or twisted to its purpose was
contemporary criticism of him as a General, one who
actually lost more battles than he won. Great as was his
popularity, it sharply fluctuated. When he lost Philadelphia
in 1777, after losing New York in 1776, it was at lowest
ebb—in contrast with that of Horatio Gates with his decisive victory at Saratoga. Criticism of him then came from
such former admirers as John Adams of Massachusetts,
Benjamin Rush of Pennsylvania, and Richard Henry Lee
of Virginia. And many an honest patriot, in and out of
Congress, at this time and later, feared that America's new
republican principles might be subverted by the people's
idolatry of him as "a Deity or Saviour." Soldiers, too, at
times thought the popular Colossus had feet of ordinary
red Virginia clay, though few were as abusive as General
Charles Lee in saying that the people's "infallible divinity"
in reality was "a bladder of emptiness and pride." Justified
or not, such criticism does reveal that Washington once
walked the earth as flesh-and-blood man. His conduct was
not always and inevitably approved; nor, when disap-
proved, was it always and exclusively by the deep-dyed
villains of the myth.

And so it was with the man as President. Few Chief
Executives have been more grossly abused by the highly
exaggerated American partisanship which has always

amazed foreigners. During his second term the Jeffersonian Republicans in full blast attacked the Father-Hero who, in their eyes, had degenerated into a partisan and senile tool of the "Anglo-monarchical Federalists." No one, for example, excelled Philip Freneau in poems exalting him as General and after his death as demigod. But at this time "The Poet of the Revolution" as a Republican editor stung the great man out of his habitual calm into one of his towering rages, in which he swore "that by God he had rather be in his grave" or back on his farm than be King of America as so falsely charged by "that rascal Freneau." No one excelled Thomas Jefferson, earlier or later, in properly appreciating Washington. But at this time, having withdrawn from the Cabinet, as Republican leader he regarded his former chief as a captive of Hamiltonian "monarchical" sycophants who utilized his godlike image to further their unholy machinations. When Washington signed Jay's Treaty with England. Jefferson privately wrote Madison that once again we must "exclaim 'curse upon his virtues, they have undone his country.'" When one such private letter, to Philip Mazzei in 1796, got into the newspapers it caused a great furore because of Jefferson's thinly-veiled reference to Washington as a political apostate, one of those "men who were Samsons in the field and Solomons in the council, but who have had their heads shorn by the harlot England."

But Jefferson was moderation itself compared to Republican editors, or to a Thomas Paine, once the watchdog of the General's reputation. Their public attacks were vicious and lacerating. As Washington himself said, they assailed him in "such exaggerated terms as could scarcely be applied to a Nero, a notorious defaulter, or even to a common pick-pocket." When he retired as President in 1797 Republican congressmen, including Andrew Jackson, refused to thank him for his services. Republican legislators of his

own Virginia debated his wisdom and patriotism. And the
nation's chief Republican editor called for a jubilee of
rejoicing "that the name of WASHINGTON from this
day ceases to give currency to political iniquity, and to
legalize corruption." Such criticism followed him into
retirement at Mount Vernon. It was active in 1798, when
once again he assumed chief military command in the
quasi-war with Revolutionary France. It pursued him into
1799, when he spoke out in defense of an American Union
he thought seriously endangered by the pro-French Republicans, and especially by the states-rights, states-inter-
position, Virginia and Kentucky Resolutions through
which Jefferson and Madison were denouncing the national
Alien and Sedition laws.

When he died in December of 1799 the myth did not at
once replace the man. Amid the eulogies of 1800 was still
heard the popular Republican toast: "George Washington
—down to the year 1787, and no farther." It was not until
Jefferson defeated Adams in that bitter presidential campaign of 1800, and the Hero of Monticello in his first
inaugural had praised the Hero of Mount Vernon as "our
first and greatest revolutionary character . . . entitled to
the first place in his country's love, and . . . the fairest
page in the volume of faithful history," that, at last, Washington was transfigured into "Freedom's myth" and "more
than man."

Federalists, to be sure, continued to exploit his godlike
image, and in a manner most revealing to the historian-
detective. John Adams himself later admitted to Jefferson
that they had done so for partisan purposes, "not that they
loved Washington." Such an exploiter was Timothy Pickering, once of Washington's Cabinet, who later privately
said of his old chief that, while he had moral integrity,
his prudence often cloaked want of decision and other
deficiencies; but "no man, however well-informed, was

willing to hazard his own popularity by exhibiting the real intellectual character of the immensely popular Washington." Robert Liston, the British Minister, early in 1800 reported that some Federalist leaders, privately, were "more inclined to depreciate his merits than to exalt his fame." Publicly, however, they had seized upon Washington Birthday eulogies as a device to foster party interests and "the formation of a *national character,* which they consider as much wanting in this country. And assuredly," said the British Minister, "the Americans will be the gainers by the periodical recital . . . of the praises of Washington. The hyperbolical amplifications of the Panegyricks in question have an evident effect . . . in fomenting the growth of that vanity, which to the feelings of a stranger, had already arrived at a sufficient height."

But as time passed panegyrics of the Father-Hero became more hyperbolical, and the extremes of adulation provoked contrary extremes. As Emerson noted, people bored by unceasing praise of him as the perfect one would often privately swear, "Damn George Washington!" Few dared publicly by voice or pen to oppose the torrents of idolatry. With rare courage Edwin P. Whipple so dared in 1850, when he said "mediocrity has a bad trick of idealizing itself in eulogizing [Washington], and drags him down to its own level" of ranting commonplaces. The sooner this popular yet preposterous image, "which its contrivers have the audacity to call George Washington, is hissed out of existence, the better." But the myth was triumphant even against the ridicule of Artemus Ward's parody of a typical eulogy: "G. Washington was abowt the best man this world ever sot eyes on. . . . He never slopt over! . . . He luved his country dearly. He wasn't after the spiles. He was a human angil in a 3 kornered hat and knee britches."

Publicly, he was as Lord Byron called him, "The Cin-

cinnatus of the West, whom Envy dared not hate." Privately, however, envy and prurience were at their foul work in the dark subterranean depths of oral tradition. Weems and Marshall might be read in the parlor but, at the other extreme, backstairs gossip developed the scandalous left-handed side of folklore. There was the obscene anecdote he allegedly told that night in the boat crossing the Delaware, a scene made famous by Leutze's popular and inaccurate painting. There were the slanders about his love affair with Sally Fairfax, wife of his best friend, his cruelty to slaves, his business dishonesty and grasping avarice, his attractive octoroon slave-girl at Mount Vernon, his mistress in New York during the war, his illegitimate son, his assignation with an overseer's wife that cold December night which brought about his fatal illness. The historian-detective finds that most of these defaming stories go back to letters forged by British and Tory propagandists during the Revolution. At that time, and later when revived against him by Jeffersonian Republicans, Washington branded them palpably false. Years ago scholars in several monographs nailed them down as untrue. But this dark image persisted, aided by new forgeries discrediting both the man and the bright image, and as late as 1929 John C. Fitzpatrick felt compelled to refute them anew in his *The George Washington Scandals*.

Rebelling against both dark and bright images, intelligent men demanded a truthful portrait, especially of his private life and character. They agreed with George William Curtis when he said a century ago that "there is nothing so deleterious to our national character . . . than to regard Washington as the Greeks did Achilles, and make him a demigod." Oddly enough, Parson Weems earlier had voiced the same demand when he criticized John Marshall's "Washingtoniad," in which "you see nothing of Washington below the *clouds*—nothing of Washington the *dutiful* son—the affectionate brother—the cheerful schoolboy—the neat draftsman—the laborious farmer—the widow's husband—the orphan's father—the poor man's friend. No! this is not the Washington you see; 'tis only Washington the HERO, and the demigod." Since the Parson himself had transformed him into Saint George and wafted him aloft through the clouds on angels' wings, this is one of the more precious bits of Weemsiana. Yet the demand he voiced grew with the passing years. Half a century later the editor of *Harper's Weekly* declared we have classic studies of "the ideal Washington, but a lifelike picture of the man as he lived, spoke, acted, thought, and demeaned himself in private, we have none."

Daring champions of "simple truth" fought—and lost—a major battle early in 1858 when they acclaimed Thackeray for his youthful Washington in *The Virginians*. While in it he plays but a minor role, it was the first attempt to present him realistically, in terms of his Virginia environment, with qualities foreshadowing his future greatness—a flesh-and-blood young man, even though one of Thackeray's characters snorted, "Hang him! he has no faults, and that's why I dislike him." Too conventional a portrait for modern tastes, it was for most Americans a century ago too shockingly unconventional. And anguished were their outcries at this sacrilege, this desecration. Most indignant was John R. Thompson, editor of Richmond's *Southern Literary Messenger*, who had just composed his most conventional Ode to Washington for the Crawford statue ceremonies. Sternly he warned Thackeray that "Washington's character has come to us spotless, and if you impute to him the little follies that have belonged to other great men, the majestic apparition you have called up may visit you, pure and white as you see him in Houdon's statue, and freeze you into silence with his calm, reproachful look." To humanize him is to falsify him, cried other

champions of the myth, as they victoriously put to rout all
who dared defend Thackeray's indecent attempt to portray Washington as other than "history proves he was, the
heaven-chosen, miraculous founder of our nation."

He was thus portrayed, as "Freedom's myth" and "more
than man," long after this battle of 1858. The man was so
obscured as to provoke the jibe that it is a wise country
that knows its own father. How ignorant and confused
Americans were about their Father-Hero was ironically
pictured in 1880 by historian Henry Adams in his novel
Democracy. Adams takes his characters from Washington
City to a picnic at Mount Vernon on a small steamer
which pounds the muddy waters of the Potomac and sends
up "its small column of smoke as if it were a newly invented incense-burner approaching the temple of the
national deity." Once there each explains what Washington means to him. A diplomat sees him "compounded of
Stuart's portrait and Greenough's statue of Olympian Jove
with Washington's features." A Virginia girl says she knows
from family tradition that he was "a raw-boned country
farmer, very hard-featured, very awkward, very illiterate
and very dull; very bad-tempered, very profane, and generally tipsy after dinner." A New England historian sees
him as "Morality, Justice, Duty, Truth; half a dozen
Roman gods with capital letters." And a brash Senator
from the West no longer sees him as the "American Je-
hovah" of his youth. having since learned that his military
and political talents at best were mediocre; inferior, indeed,
to a dozen public men then adorning that epoch of President Rutherford B. Hayes.

Henry Adams in 1880 was far from exaggerating the
confusion of Americans as to the Father of their country.
Five years later another historian, John B. McMaster, said
that "the outlines of his biography are known to every
schoolboy in the land, yet his true biography is yet to be

prepared. General Washington is known to us, and President Washington. But George Washington is an unknown man." Thirty-two years later, in the second decade of the twentieth century, another major historian, Edward Channing, voiced the same conclusion: "As to the inner man we are even now strangely ignorant. No more elusive personality exists in history."

Even in this sixth decade of the twentieth century these same remarks have been repeated by some historians reviewing Douglas Southall Freeman's recent multi-volumed biography of Washington. Still to be heard is the remark of 1858 that to humanize him is to falsify him. And in 1958 Marcus Cunliffe in his *George Washington, Man and Monument* came to the conclusion that it is now impossible to separate the man from the myth: for "the man *is* the monument; the monument *is* America."

This pays much too high a tribute to the myth with its de-humanizing abstractions and symbolisms. Admittedly the line between myth and reality, though often very broad, is sometimes narrow, and symbols in varying degree do have a basis in actualities. But this does not excuse the historian from his responsibility to separate fact from over-blown fancy to the utmost of his fallible abilities. Alas, while history does not repeat itself, historians often repeat one another. Yet to repeat McMaster and Channing at this late day is to jettison impressive recent scholarship on Washington, and on the men and events of his epoch. For the historian to do so is abjectly to embrace the opposing concept of the poet, to whom myth is the supreme reality because, true or false, that is what people believe.

Back in the 1930s when simple truth was roughly jostling the demigod image, Gertrude Stein was less than successful in defending the myth when she wrote "George Washington was and is the father of his country," and he "may easily have come and gone also have gone also have come.

. . . Please do not let me wander. She is very sleepy. George
Washington." More intelligible was Donald Davidson's
defense of the poet's concept when he then said: "George
Washington grows ever more faint and far away for most
Americans as the image of Washington built in the homely
glorification of the Parson Weems tradition is dissected
and cast aside, and as the man . . . is more and more in-
sisted upon by the historian . . . . We have lately freshened
our knowledge of Washington, but it cannot be said that
we have thereby quickened our feeling for him as a hero."

The last three decades have indeed "freshened our
knowledge of Washington." Unlike Thackeray in 1858,
those in the 1920s who began to emphasize the man rather
than the myth were aided by a favorable climate of opinion. A more matured America was more receptive to their
war cry of "Pedestals are made for statues, not for men."
Even so, that overzealous warrior, W. E. Woodward, in
1926 felt compelled to use the shock-tactics of debunking,
and with much justice was accused of being a Weems in
reverse. Far more important was Rupert Hughes, who by
his realistic approach pioneered the way for many others,
most notably Douglas Southall Freeman. In spite of anguished outcries, Hughes with a heavy machete slashed
away at the lush and obscuring Weemsian jungle, and as
the merits of the man were more clearly revealed the
higher mounted his admiration. Freeman's seven volumes,
the last written by his collaborators, have been justly
acclaimed as a landmark, though they lack the full character analysis he planned for his final volume and probably "dulcify" relatively few general readers by their
exhaustive and exhausting detail. But by his scholarly
detail he has provided the Washington sourcebook for
current biographies, and by his sympathetic yet realistic
portrayal of the man has pointed the way for the many
more biographies yet to be written.

But this is to note only the high spots in a remarkable shift of emphasis from the myth to the man. Since Mr. Davidson made his observation in the 1930s there has been a veritable flood of books which as to scholarship and content have met the insistent demands of the historian. They have sought to present all phases of the man's life in terms of human experience. They have sought to evaluate more precisely his public services by placing them in their historical setting. In their efforts they have been greatly aided by the renaissance in Revolutionary studies with its many monographs, and by the many recent scholarly biographies of Washington's colleagues and opponents. And all this has measurably corrected, chastened, and at times unmercifully flayed that preposterous popular image which as early as 1850 Edwin P. Whipple would have hissed out of existence. Poets and professional patrioteers may lament this dissecting and deflating of the myth. But historians and all devoted to Abigail Adams' "simple truth" are indeed grateful that at last justice is being done to a great and good man. Instead of the demigod of Parson Weems and Company we now have increasingly a more human, a more credible, and a far more inspiring Washington.

In its monolithic simplicity the man's character, to be sure, will always challenge any biographer. For simplicity can be more baffling than subtlety. One of the most perceptive of the many attempts to depict his character was made by James Russell Lowell, who with rare insight emphasized the man's solid, untheatrical, and in times of crisis inspiring qualities as the hard-won fruits of self-discipline. For here, said Lowell, was "a man for men . . . no more a pallid image and a dream —

> . . . This balanced soul
> So simple in its grandeur, coldly bare
> Of draperies theatric, standing there

In perfect symmetry of self-control,
Seems not so great at first, but greater grows
Still as we look, and by experience learn
How grand this quiet is, how nobly stern
The discipline that wrought through lifelong throes
That energetic passion of repose.

Only rarely did Washington in his many letters reveal his innermost thoughts. But the historian-detective finds one such letter that may be used as a key to his character and a measure of his greatness. It was written to a lifelong friend on January 20, 1799, just five days after he had urged Patrick Henry back into politics to defend what he called "everything most sacred and dear." Bryan Fairfax, resenting partisan abuse of him during the French crisis, had assured him that old friends warmly praised him for once again leaving Mount Vernon to assume chief military command. In reply Washington thanked Fairfax, and said such sentiments could only be pleasing to a man who through life had "always walked on a straight line, and endeavoured as far as human frailties, and perhaps strong passions, would enable him, to discharge the relative duties to his Maker and fellow-men, without seeking any indirect or lefthanded attempts to acquire popularity."

These few words are revealing of the man, so long obscured by the myth. To an extraordinary degree he had through life "always walked on a straight line," whether as a young colonial officer, Squire of Mount Vernon, Commander-in-chief, or first President. As a youth he had adopted that straight-line code of the Virginia gentleman. He was then, as we now know, intensely ambitious for wealth and glory; a hard-driving, very emotional young man who, for example, on his first campaign naively exulted in what he called the "charming" sound of whistling bullets. We can now see more clearly how that rawboned youth gradually evolved into the "balanced soul of simple

grandeur," his ambitions transmuted into channels so
beneficial to his country in war and peace. It is inspiring
to observe that process of self-discipline, and the maturing
effects of grave responsibilities always willingly assumed,
by which he grew to that high moral stature for which as
General and President he is justly admired. And we admire him the more when we see him as he really was, a
fallible man, yet one who had indubitably made himself
the commanding figure in an epoch of great men.

Not by mythic magic had he done this but by human
effort. A slow-but-sure man, without the warmth and popular qualities of a Patrick Henry or the depth and penetration of a many-sided Thomas Jefferson, he had made
the most of what he modestly called his "inferior endow-
ments" inherited from nature; he had mastered to a degree
his "human frailties," and he had attained a remarkable
though never perfect control over his admitted "strong
passions."

It is this flesh-and-blood man we can now appreciate far
more than "Freedom's myth." Before his marriage he
really was in love with Sally Fairfax, but he had sufficient
character to avoid any impropriety. He was whole-heart-
edly devoted to his Mount Vernon home, to the theatre,
dancing, and the sports of turf and field. Though he had
little humor he was not devoid of it, and could joke about
the frigid indifference to Virginia's mares of Royal Gift,
the jackass given him by the King of Spain. As Commander-in-chief he was capable of graciously returning to General Sir William Howe his little pet dog that had wandered
off into no-man's land. In the war he was only one-tenth
able field commander but nine-tenths great administrator.
While he surmounted almost insuperable obstacles, his
head was never turned by a grateful people's idolatry. Yet
with all his superb self-control he keenly resented criticism,
as he did in 1777 when, after losing Philadelphia, some

men loosely talked of replacing him. Though the so-called
Conway Cabal against him at that time is now thought to
be much less than the villainous conspiracy of tradition,
his anger and indignation then was very human indeed.

As President he was no demigod, but neither was he a
mere front man for Alexander Hamilton as he so often
appears in biographies of both Hamilton and Jefferson.
When these two great men served in his Cabinet he was
in truth their leader. He ably utilized their genius for a
new nation then embarked on a precarious experiment,
based on the radical idea that the people are sovereign and
are capable of self-government without kings or dictators.
Yet we now know that he did increasingly become a Federalist partisan. He never seemed quite to understand the
emerging party system, and was too prone to regard as dis-
loyalty to America that honest criticism of governmental
measures so vitally necessary in a democracy. But above all
we can now see more clearly his invaluable contributions.
With his unrivalled prestige, he worked most effectively
to bring about the Constitution of 1787. And no man
equalled him, during his eight critical years as President,
in making the Constitution's new government a well-
established reality. By so doing he utterly confounded the
many cynics at home and in monarchical Europe who had
predicted that republican America's hard-won independence would in the end prove a curse rather than a bless-
ing. In peace as in war, he was truly "The Anchor of
American Union."

As the man emerges from the long-obscuring myth he
comes more closely to resemble the miniature portrait
carefully drawn of him in 1814 by Thomas Jefferson. Of
all attempts to depict his character this is by far the most
perceptive and balanced, because based on intimate knowledge and simple truth. In describing a Washington with
whom he had once differed — as to methods but never as he

said in a common devotion to the rights of man — and with whom he had long served, in Virginia under Patrick Henry's leadership, then in Congress and in the Cabinet, Jefferson was writing a page in what he once called "the volume of faithful history":

His mind was great and powerful, without being of the very first order; his penetration strong, though not so acute as that of a Newton, Bacon, or Locke; and as far as he saw, no judgment was ever sounder. It was slow in operation, being little aided by invention or imagination, but sure in conclusion. . . . Perhaps the strongest feature in his character was prudence, never acting until every circumstance, every consideration, was maturely weighed; refraining if he saw a doubt, but, when once decided, going through with his purpose whatever obstacles opposed. His integrity was most pure, his justice the most inflexible I have ever known, no motives of interest or consanguinity, of friendship or hatred, being able to bias his decision. He was, indeed, in every sense of the words, a wise, a good, and a great man.

His temper was naturally irritable and high toned; but reflection and resolution had obtained a firm and habitual ascendency over it. If ever, however, it broke its bonds, he was most tremendous in his wrath. In his expenses he was honorable, but exact; liberal in contributions to whatever promised utility; but frowning . . . on . . . all unworthy calls on his charity. His heart was not warm in its affections; but he exactly calculated every man's value, and gave him a solid esteem proportioned to it. His person . . . was fine, his stature exactly what one would wish, his deportment easy, erect and noble; the best horseman of his age, and the most graceful figure that could be seen on horseback. Although in the circle of his friends, where he might be unreserved with safety, he took a free share in conversation, his colloquial talents were not above mediocrity, possessing neither copiousness of ideas, nor fluency of words. In public, when called on for a sudden opinion, he was unready, short and embarrassed. Yet he wrote readily, rather diffusely, in an easy and correct style. This he had acquired by conversation with the world, for his education was merely reading, writing, and common arithmetic, to which he added surveying at a later day. His time was employed in action chiefly, reading little, and that only in agriculture and English history. . . .

On the whole his character was, in its mass, perfect, in nothing bad, in few points indifferent; and it may truly be said, that never did nature and fortune combine more perfectly to make a man great, and to place him in the same constellation with whatever worthies have merited from man an everlasting remembrance. For his was the singular destiny and merit of leading the armies of his country successfully through an arduous war for the establishment of its independence; of conducting its councils through the birth of a government, new in its forms and principles, until it had settled down into a quiet and orderly train; and of scrupulously obeying the laws through the whole of his career, civil and military, of which the history of the world furnishes no other example.

LECTURE

THREE

The Strange Case of Thomas Jefferson

IN FEBRUARY OF 1858 WHEN PATRIOTIC PILGRAMS BRAVED A driving snowstorm for the unveiling in Richmond of Crawford's statues of George Washington, Patrick Henry, and Thomas Jefferson, historian Hugh Blair Grigsby was one of the many orators who extolled these heroes as The Sword, The Trumpet, and The Pen of the Revolution. In the beautiful Greek temple Capitol designed by Jefferson he expressed his "grateful and affectionate veneration" of all three Virginians whom Thomas Crawford had honored "with the eternal voice of sculpture." But it was Thomas Jefferson whom he held in highest esteem, since above all other Founding Fathers "his history is indeed the history of American liberty."

In thus exalting him a century ago Grigsby was then in a decided minority, strange as this may seem today when Jefferson is so generally acclaimed, so conspicuously a part of our American heritage. Yet in his time and down into ours Jefferson's reputation has been one of sharply conflicting bright and dark images. His popular image is very bright today, but this is the result of a victory only recently won by his admirers in a long-sustained battle with his many detractors.

The lines of that battle were clearly marked in 1858 when Henry S. Randall published his classic three-volume biography of Jefferson. His reputation, as Randall noted, was "more assailed by class and hereditary hate than . . . all others belonging to our early history — scarcely defended by a page where volumes have been written to traduce it." On the other hand his reputation was "resistlessly spreading, until all parties seek to appropriate it — until not an American . . . dare place himself before a popular constituency with revilings of Jefferson on his lips." Yet in 1858 there also appeared Samuel M. Schmucker's biography of him which, strangely enough, darkened rather than brightened his reputation. Widely read and destined to go into several printings, it portrayed a Jefferson who had "a pusillanimous and morbid terror of popular censure, and an insatiable thirsting after popular praise." It well illustrated what Randall called "the leering, sneering" manner "which has been so extensively practised by early and late calumniators of Mr. Jefferson."

Since the forces of darkness were then so powerful, it is not strange that Grigsby in 1858 rapturously hailed Randall's biography as the "first great defence in the forum of history of our noble chief of Monticello." For refuting the many works defaming him, "every liberal American ought to thank you," wrote Virginia's leading historian to the New York biographer. "No Virginian could have written the life of Jefferson," since even here in Virginia, even among his own Randolph kin, he still has many "bitter and unappeasable enemies." Regardless of hostile reviewers, wrote Grigsby consolingly, "be assured that your day of triumph will come; but whether the time be long or short, I am not able to say."

Far less consoling were letters to Randall from England's leading historian, Lord Macaulay. Randall's excellent biography had failed to change Macaulay's preference for the conservative views of Washington. It had failed to soften Macaulay's stinging indictment of a Jefferson whose democratic principles, so His Lordship grimly predicted, would by our day cause a "fatal calamity" and destroy America. "Your republic will be as fearfully plundered and laid waste in the twentieth century as the Roman Empire was in the fifth," he wrote Randall. "Your Huns and Vandals will have been engendered within your own country by your own institutions. Thinking thus, of course I can not reckon Jefferson among the benefactors of mankind." While "your institutions have, during the whole of the nineteenth century, been constantly becoming more Jeffersonian and less Washingtonian," said Macaulay, "it is surely strange that while this process has been going on, Washington should have been exalted into a god, and Jefferson degraded into a demon."

In reporting The Strange Case of Thomas Jefferson the historian-detective finds it pleasing to note that the republic has survived to become the democratic leader of a free world which includes Macaulay's England. But to explain Jefferson's dark image is less pleasing, since it suggests that to be great is to be misunderstood, and to be great in American politics is to be grossly abused. For his strange case is unparalleled for its vilification, and for the use and misuse of a great man's reputation.

His degrading into a demon is directly connected with the exalting of Washington into a god by Parson Weems, John Marshall, and innumerable other biographers. The Father of His Country was long pictured as divinely ordained. Weems, for example, in his many best-selling editions carried him aloft to Heaven on angels' wings, and when Crawford's statues were unveiled, though Jefferson was praised, Washington was sanctified as "the Messiah of

the land" with Virginia as his "Bethlehem." In this de-
ifying process Washington's colleagues were glorified and
his opponents damned. Alexander Hamilton became his
Federalist archangel; Jefferson as his chief Republican opponent became a demoniac Satan.

For years after Washington's death his godlike image
was exploited for anti-Jefferson purposes by the Hamil-
tonians. As Washington's diabolical rival, Jefferson was
condemned in the many biographies of Washington, Hamilton, and other Federalist heroes on down into our time,
in the partisan tradition of Marshall's Washington. This
work by Jefferson's cousin, the Chief Justice, published
when Jefferson was President and denounced by him as a
Federalist libel, long served Americans as a political history. Today Satan's tail does not twitch so violently, and
the smell of brimstone is not so overpowering. But the
Jefferson of Federalist tradition appeared conspicuously in
Albert J. Beveridge's life of John Marshall. As such he was
subjected to the righteous scorn of John C. Fitzpatrick in
his 1933 biography idealizing Washington. And some
scholars have detected a whiff of sulphur, a twitching of
the tail, in the seventh volume of Freeman's Washington,
written by Freeman's collaborators and published in 1957.

This degrading process was given impetus in Jefferson's
lifetime by his success in advancing democratic principles,
a success so marked that the Federalists became the most
frustrated politicians in our history. Self-styled "the rich,
wise, well-born, and able," they believed that they alone
should rule. To them the word "democracy" was a nasty
word, akin to "mobocracy" and "anarchy." As such the
word was employed by Hamilton when he called on conventional religion and entrenched wealth to save America
from Jefferson's "poison of democracy." Washington used
it and the equally nasty word "Jacobin," akin today to
"Communist," in denouncing Jefferson's criticism of such

reactionary policies as the Sedition Law, by which the Federalists would throttle all political criticism. Throughout Jefferson's presidency, for example, America's foremost magazine editor, Joseph Dennie of the *Port Folio,* with almost incredible scurrility each week pilloried and ridiculed that "Mammoth of Democracy" in the White House. And as early as 1804 he anticipated Lord Macaulay by declaring that "the fever of Democracy," by corrupting politics and morals, had all but pushed the republic into "the grave which Anarchy is digging for our Commonwealth."

Dennie was but one of a dark legion of contemporary writers, politicians, and conservative clergymen dedicated to the degradation of Thomas Jefferson. For years they assailed him in a manner that made Republican abuse of Washington pale into insignificance. They blackened his image by many a slanderous untruth. He was an atheist, they said, an infidel member of that unholy trinity of "Tom Paine, Tom Jefferson, and Tom the Devil." He was a libertine slaveholder with mulatto children by "Monticellian Black Sally," so widely and so falsely publicized in prose and verse. He was a coward, they said, who as war governor fled so precipitately when the British took Charlottesville. His critics overlooked, as did historian Edward Channing lecturing at Harvard in our time on the affrighted Jefferson "coattails flying in the wind," that Patrick Henry also preferred liberty to death, wisely deciding with Jefferson not to fight the British army single-handedly.

This "cowardly wretch" was an impractical visionary, they said, who as President failed to act with vigor and decision. Yet when he so acted, he was an oppressive tyrant, the devil incarnate. His two "vile administrations," according to Timothy Pickering of Massachusetts, for example, were marked by "prevarication, duplicity, and

sophistry." Jefferson himself, said this diehard Hamiltonian Federalist, was "the arch-juggler" and "a miserable,
skulking projector"; he was "our Great Land-Jobber" as
to Louisiana, a cunning manipulator of "dupes and pup-
pets," a deceiving demagogue who always put popularity
above principle, "the most flagitious of public men," and
above all for "the wise and good," the Federalists, "their
greatest, their exterminating enemy."

He was darkly portrayed as a ferocious "Frenchified
Jacobin," with all the overtones of French Revolutionary
excesses, lusting to chop off heads in the name of Human-
ity and the Age of Reason. Yet he was, as well, the pen-
sioned and cringing slave of despotic Emperor Napoleon.
He was as famous for his French red breeches and crack-
pot inventions as for the "glittering generalities" of his
Declaration of Independence; "that false, and flatulent,
and foolish" Declaration about liberty and equality, said
Editor Dennie, the public reading of which each July 4th
should be banned since it only inflamed the masses and
gave them ideas above their proper station in life. He was
a man befogged by metaphysical contraditions, with vain
and silly pretensions to universal knowledge. He was most
absurd when spouting forth his moonshine philosophy
about the inalienable rights of all men. Only a hypocritical
demagogue, they said, could so obstinately profess his faith
in the virtue and capacity for advancement of "our American peasantry." For every gentleman not a renegade to his
class must agree with Hamilton that Jefferson's beloved
homespun people was a many-headed monster, a dangerous
and fearsome beast.

Yet dark as was this image pictured by his enemies, in
his lifetime the bright image predominated. The evidence
is overwhelming. It is attested by his election as Vice President in 1796, his defeat of John Adams in the presidential
contest of 1800, and by his landslide victory in 1804 when,

with moderate Federalists and independent voters flocking
to his standard, he carried all seventeen states of the Union
except Connecticut and Delaware. He refused to consider
a third term. But his Virginia Dynasty of national Republican leadership continued on for sixteen more years under
his lieutenants Madison and Monroe. As Macaulay noted,
America constantly became more democratic, more Jeffersonian.

Jefferson's faith in the people had been returned in
good measure at the polls. Though "a fair mark for every
man's dirt," as he said, he had so conducted himself in
public and private as to transform many former opponents into warm friends. Such was the case with Senator
William Plumer, Federalist of New Hampshire, when he
had "the more critically and impartially" examined "the
character and conduct of Mr. Jefferson." And Margaret
Bayard Smith of Washington marveled that the real man
was so unlike the partisan caricatures that had frightened
her Federalist family. It was impossible to believe, she
said, that "this man so meek and mild, yet dignified in his
manners, with a voice so soft and low, with a countenance
so benignant and intelligent" could be "the violent democrat, the vulgar demagogue, the bold atheist and profligate
man I have so often heard denounced." She became convinced, almost to the point of idolatry, as did most Americans that Thomas Jefferson was "truly a philosopher, and
truly a good man, and eminently a great one."

In spite of his many broadcloth enemies, he was indeed
the homespun people's beloved President. Republican editors, orators, and liberal clergymen — ever grateful to him
as the champion of religious freedom — more than held
their own in combatting his foes and extravagantly prais-
ing him to the skies. Typical was John Beckley's widely
reprinted pamphlet biography of 1800, in which one by
one he refuted Federalist charges and slanders. These he

attributed to their jealousy of his unrivalled and many-
sided talents; to their fear that as President "every germ of
monarchy and aristocracy . . . will dissipate at the electri-
cal touch of his republican virtues"; and to their anger
"that notwithstanding all their distractious efforts, he continues to possess the unshaken and undiminished confi-
dence of the great body of the American people." For the
people know him well as "a man of pure, ardent, and un-
affected piety; . . . of an enlightened mind and superior
wisdom; the adorer of our God; the patriot of his country; and the friend and benefactor of the whole human
race."

For years this bright image was presented in hamlets
from Maine to Georgia, from seaport towns to frontier
clearings. In many a song "Columbia's sons" rejoiced that
to tyrants they would never bend the knee, but always
"join with heart and soul and voice, for Jefferson and
Liberty." Proudly they sang of "The People's Friend"
divinely ordained to safeguard and to advance the hard-
won gains of the American Revolution; a Jefferson "employed by Heaven" itself to write with his "hallowed Pen"
the Declaration of Independence and thereafter ensure
"the Rights of Man and Equal Laws."

On the Fourth of July, his day of days and later consecrated by his death, citizens participated in the standard
patriotic ritual. They paraded to the stirring strains of
"Jefferson's March." They respectfully listened to the reading of his ever-inspiring Declaration of 1776. They then
heard a perfervid oration which lavished homage on him
as the Philosopher-Sage of Monticello, the Versatile Genius, the Pontifex Maximus of pure republicanism, against
whom "the arts of malice and the rude voice of faction
assail . . . in vain." Like Cato, he was devoted to his country; like Socrates, his affections embraced the universe;
like Jupiter on Olympus, he surveyed with serenity and

silence the awful fate of Old World aristocracy and monarchy.

Jefferson's own mythology became impressive. But hero-
worshipping Americans then or later never quite deified
him as they did Washington. He had no Weems to waft
him aloft on angels' wings. He never became devitalized
into a collection of abstract virtues, a demigod aloof from
the everyday realities of American life. Unlike Washington, he was too vividly human, too warm and many-sided
a spirit, ever to be congealed into marble. In his own day,
as he was to become in ours, he was the supreme symbol
of democracy. And if as a folk-hero he was second to
Washington, symbol of national union and moral perfection, his was always a more provocative symbol. For in his
lifetime, and long after, the bright myth of popular admiration had to contend with the dark myth of partisan
condemnation.

Even in retirement he was made acutely aware of this
conflicting dark image. He was still the whipping boy and
bogeyman for his traducers, as he wryly said in 1810, even
after serving them "faithfully for . . . years in the terrific
station of Rawhead and Bloodybones." The dark image
was magnified during the War of 1812 by anti-war New
England Federalists, led by Timothy Pickering and Josiah
Quincy. Such men talked of disunion and vilified Jefferson as the root cause of all their woes. In his defense
Henry Clay, in one of the most eloquent speeches of his
career, painted such a bright picture of him that he moved
Republican congressmen to tears, and so effectively stung
the Federalists that for weeks thereafter they jeered at
Clay as "Jefferson's Knight of the Red Breeches."

In postwar years he was assured by John Adams, now
reconciled with his old colleague of 1776, that the partisan
"ass has kicked in vain." But Jefferson, still troubled,
sought to defend his reputation by preparing his letters

for future publication. In February of 1826, in his eighty-third year, when his usual optimism was sorely tried by heavy debts, he wrote a revealing letter to James Madison. He was solacing himself, the old gentleman wrote, with the belief that Madison was writing a history to confound their persistent enemies. He was sure this would vindicate "to posterity the course we have pursued for preserving to them, in all their purity, the blessings of self-government, which we had assisted too in acquiring for them. If ever the earth has beheld a system of administration conducted with a single and steadfast eye to the general interest and happiness . . . it is that to which our lives have been devoted. To myself you have been a pillar of support through life. Take care of me when dead, and be assured that I shall leave with you my last affections."

When he died a few months later, on July 4th, 1826, his image flamed brightly. A nation celebrating on that same day its Jubilee of the 50th anniversary of his Declaration of Independence marveled at this miraculous coincidence. It was made even more singular by the death of John Adams on that same Fourth of July. Both Adams and the Author of the Great Declaration for months thereafter were fulsomely eulogized by countless orators. The country has gone "Commemoration Mad!" exclaimed old Timothy Pickering, who detested both Adams and Jefferson; even some Federalists have joined in this "present popular mania" for extolling "the Moonshine philosopher of Monticello." It seemed in 1826 that this "Heaven-sent union" in death of Federalist John Adams and Republican Thomas Jefferson was a God-given sign. America's Revolutionary Epoch was now closed. Old partisan rivalries were at last ended. A new age had dawned in which only the virtues of a dead Jefferson, now enshrined with the deified Washington, would henceforth be commemorated.

But The Strange Case of Thomas Jefferson was far from

being closed. Old John Adams spoke truly when on his
deathbed he muttered, "Thomas Jefferson still lives." For
three years later, when four volumes of his papers were
published, Jefferson spoke out from the grave, and with
explosive effect. Very frankly written, in all "the warmth
and freshness of fact and feeling" of the moment, as he
once said, his letters gave his wide-ranging views on most
of the controversial issues of America's first fifty years of
quick-changing development. Men of the Federalist tradition cried out in anguish at his criticisms of the sainted
Washington, of Hamilton and other opponents. To combat him they published defensive and partisan biographies
and writings. And thus Jefferson still lived on, in a re-
newed battle of contending mythologies.

Even more significant was the use and misuse of his
bright image by partisan rivals who would exploit his
name and fame. His writings of 1829, and a fuller edition
of 1853, became like the Bible an arsenal of arguments
from which men of opposing views selected, and excluded,
what suited their own purposes. In thus seizing upon his
opinions which supported, or seemed to support, what
they themselves advocated, they made him a football of
partisan politics. They obscured the real man, and dam-
aged his reputation by making him appear to sustain every
side of every question, to appear all things to all men.

The Jacksonian Democrats, for example, claimed him as
their very own, and used his views to support their laissez-
faire, states rights and, on occasion, nationalistic policies.
In this they vied with Clay's National Republicans, later
known as Whigs, who also claimed him as their party
symbol. At the same time he was claimed by Calhoun's
anti-national Nullifiers of South Carolina, despite Madison's sharp protest that Calhoun was perverting not only
the states rights views Jefferson and himself had expressed
in the Virginia and Kentucky Resolutions of 1798 but

Jefferson's basic and vital principle of majority rule.

Champions of the Old South used his states rights views as a defensive weapon. But they rejected as "glittering generalities" his basic principles of the Declaration of Independence that "all men are created equal" and have inalienable rights. Abolitionists abused him as a slaveholder. But they made effective use of his inalienable rights and his many denunciations of slavery. The Democratic party long used him as its father-image. But it was challenged by the new major party formed in 1854 which appropriated the very name of his old Republican party. Its chieftain, Abraham Lincoln, a democratic nationalist in the Clay tradition, held high the banner of a Jefferson whose principles, he declared, "are the definitions and axioms of free society . . . applicable to all men and all times." But against Lincoln, Southerners who in the 1860s fought for their independence cited as precedent Jefferson's Declaration of 1776, which had justified secession from Britain.

As a result of this confusion of symbols and myths, this welter of half-truths and distortions, the frankly-spoken, complex, and many-sided Jefferson was made to appear the most inconsistent of men. Of his many symbols which partisans used, and misused, most firmly established was that of states rights, with its various connotations. When states rights with its connotations of nullification and disunion met defeat at Appomattox his popularity declined. It was low in the Age of Big Business and of Robber Barons, which made Hamilton its hero. In the conservative Age of William McKinley his reputation was such that William E. Curtis, in his rather oddly entitled *The True Thomas Jefferson* of 1901, gave serious attention to those who compared him unfavorably as a statesman even to a General Grant.

Most surprising in this Strange Case of Thomas Jefferson is to find his dark image predominating in the liberal

Age of the Progressive Movement. The man had become obscured indeed by conflicting myths, his basic philosophy fragmentized and twisted out of context. His states rights symbol as one connoting laissez-faire negativism, opposed to using national power for the national good, was so rigidly established that he was unappreciated by a Woodrow Wilson and despised by a Theodore Roosevelt. Both of these progressives sought to reach goals which in reality were those of Jefferson. Yet both praised not Jefferson but Hamilton, whose nationalistic methods they used to attain their Jeffersonian ends. Wilson thought Hamilton "easily the ablest" of the Founding Fathers. Roosevelt could say nothing harsher of William Jennings Bryan than that he was as "cheap and shallow" as Thomas Jefferson. And Herbert Croly, brain-truster for the Progressive Epoch, likewise condemned his "intellectual superficiality and insincerity." Even darker was his image in the conservative Age of Calvin Coolidge. All too typical was the address given at Mr. Jefferson's University of Virginia in the 1920s by Secretary of State Frank B. ("Nervous Nellie") Kellogg, in which he said that while Jefferson was a great man and all that, his ideas were dangerously radical.

Yet it was in these same 1920s that the day of triumph predicted in 1858 by Grigsby at last began to dawn for his "noble chief of Monticello." That bright dawn was heralded in 1925 by Claude G. Bowers' partisan and popular *Jefferson and Hamilton*. While it glorified Jefferson, it was a refreshing antidote to the many volumes then exalting Hamilton as the hero of an epoch typified by Coolidge's remark that "the business of America is business." A movement then began which has so brightened Jefferson's popular image, not as a partisan hero but as the supreme symbol of democracy, that today he equals, and for many even eclipses, Washington as a national hero. That movement gathered impetus in the New Deal 1930s,

reached a peak in the Jefferson Bicentennial of wartime
1943, and still retains its momentum in the cold war 1950s.

Jefferson has been honored by a magnificent memorial
in Washington. His Monticello, for a century neglected
and its tombstone mutilated, is now restored as a shrine to
which come each year over 250,000 patriotic pilgrims.
Volume after volume of his writings superbly edited by
Julian P. Boyd are coming off the press to be met with
critical acclaim. Monograph after monograph by numerous
scholars have revealed almost every phase of his many-
faceted career. And of the many recent biographies, that in
progress by Dumas Malone, by its detailed and judicious
scholarship promises to do for our appreciative generation
what Randall's classic work of 1858 did for earlier and
unappreciative Americans.

Because of this impressive recent scholarship the man
as reality rather than myth is much more clearly seen, even
though popular adulation tends to obscure that reality.
Democratic orators at fund-raising Jefferson Day Dinners
contribute richly more often to mythology than to history.
Partisan writers sometimes have made him more of a New
Dealer than Franklin D. Roosevelt. And Isom R. Lamb
of California, strangely enough, by a Bridey Murphy hyp-
notic trance regression has communicated directly with
him; from the spirit world he reports that all accounts
except his own forthcoming book are inadequate portray-
als of the heroic Sage of Monticello. Even more interesting
to the historian-detective are the excesses and distortions
of conservatives. The popular tide has overwhelmed all
their attempts to exploit both his image and a dead past—
whether it was the "Liberty Leaguers" of the 1930s, the
states rights "Jeffersonian Democrats" of the 1940s, or the
pro-segregation "Defenders of State Sovereignty and Individual Liberties" of the 1950s. Most interesting to observe
have been today's ineffectual "New Conservatives," who

lament the death in our time of a Jefferson shaped in their own anti-liberal image. Like Macaulay and their Federalist predecessors they grimly predict that the "New Jefferson" now so popular is a democratic demon who will destroy the republic.

In this latest chapter of The Strange Case of Thomas Jefferson perhaps these present-day Macaulays, in their lefthanded manner, pay him the greatest of tributes. For a vital and living Jefferson has at last triumphed in the long battle waged by his admirers over his detractors. His bright image predominates today because he is so conspicuously a part of our continuing and usable American heritage. It predominates because in our critical epoch, as in his own Age of Anxiety and social upheaval, the democracy he symbolizes has been severely tested, thus far successfully, by economic depression, world war, and today's struggle against totalitarian tyranny. By deepening our knowledge of him, and of the men and events of his Revolutionary Epoch, recent and extensive scholarship has revealed him to be the most contemporary of the Founding Fathers, as best symbolizing the ideals of both the Revolution and of present-day democracy. Jefferson still lives, as John Adams truly said, because he dealt with basic issues as pertinent to free society in our day as in his, and in timeless manner still speaks with inspiring eloquence for that democracy we would preserve and advance.

Our appreciation of him as a contemporary comrade-in-arms is not lessened by seeing him as he really was, a great though fallible man. He himself disliked what he called the "fan-coloring biographers" of his own day who exalted men into gods. We now know that he was very human indeed. Warmly affectionate with family and friends, he had a pervasive kindness, a generous richness of heart and mind, that charmed and enchanted such a Federalist as Margaret Bayard Smith. He was keenly sensitive to criti-

cism, though in public with more than Christian forbear-
ance he turned the other cheek to his relentless enemies.
Yet in his warm and unguarded letters he himself was
often sharply critical and zealously partisan.

In them he often made such sweeping statements as the
tree of liberty from time to time must be manured with
the blood of tyrants, or the French Revolution was justified if it left alive only an Adam and an Eve to continue a
race of free men. Though in action a moderate, he thus
exposed himself to criticism as an extremist. "If he had
more of General Washington's reserve," said his admiring
friend William Wirt, "he would be less in the power of his
enemies than he is." The judicious Madison, most intimate
of the "numerous and able coadjutors" to whom he gave
such generous credit, did much to temper his impulsive
tendencies. As Madison said after his letters were published, "allowances . . . ought to be made for a habit in
Mr. Jefferson, as in others of great genius, of expressing in
strong and round terms, impressions of the moment."

He was very human in his zealous partisanship which,
for example, darkened Patrick Henry's reputation and
helped establish the still flourishing myth that Washington's Federalists were "Monarchists." While often indirect
in his political tactics, preferring flanking operations to
frontal attacks, we now know how untrue was the Federalists' picture of him as a detestable and hypocritical demagogue. We know also how their persistent myth that he was
more pro-French than pro-American has been put to scorn
by scholars who portray him as the unrivalled "Apostle of
Americanism." When most furiously assailed as a "Frenchified Jacobin" for opposing Jay's Treaty with England, the
French Minister made this report on him to Revolutionary
Paris: today "Mr. Jefferson likes us because he detests
England . . . but tomorrow he might change his opinion
about us if England should cease to inspire his fear" for

America's interests. "Although Jefferson is the friend of"
a France dedicated to liberty, equality, and fraternity,
above all else "Jefferson, I say, is an American."

We now appreciate better not only how zealous he was
but how pragmatically flexible, how amazingly versatile
and complex. The complexity of his character and personality explains why biographers find him most difficult
to present full-bodied and why rival partisans in exploiting
his fame have made him appear inconsistent. It is most
naive, though not uncommon, to be surprised that his
views changed from 1769, when as a British colonist he
entered public life, to his death on the 50th anniversary
of American independence some sixty years later. It would
be surprising indeed not to find changes. Like all public
men he worked under the pressures of events and of other
human beings. And of course there were cleavages between
ideals and realities—human gaps between ideal solutions
and those he could obtain only through practical politics;
between the Sage of Monticello and the party leader; between professions out of power and actions in power; between the humanitarian who often said "Peace is my passion" and the rebel of 1776 who in 1801 fought the pirates
of Tripoli and in 1812 approved America's Second War
for Independence.

What greatly impresses the historian-detective is Jefferson's remarkable consistency, his lifelong devotion to
his basic principles of the freedom and happiness of man—
of the liberty of the individual and, since "all men are
created equal" and live in society, of the social welfare.
Liberty and equality were fundamentally moral principles.
They were "self-evident truths" deeply rooted in "the laws
of Nature and of Nature's God." Life and liberty were
inseparable, he said, for "the God who gave us life gave
us liberty at the same time; the hand of force may destroy
but cannot disjoin them." And always with Jefferson the

measure of an individual was the good he contributes to
society: for "Nature has implanted in our breasts a love
of others, a sense of duty to them, a moral instinct; in
short . . . Nature has constituted *utility* to man the standard and test of virtue." Democracy's great task is to recon-
cile the individualistic principle of liberty with the social
principle of equality.

In the past Jefferson's insistence upon individual freedom has often been distorted into the near-anarchy of a
selfish "rugged individualism." In our time his insistence
upon the social welfare has been much better appreciated,
much more emphasized, by a democratic people compelled
to use increasingly its national government in solving
problems of national security and of an America urbanized
and industrialized. In our time, also, we find perhaps the
strangest aspect of The Strange Case of Thomas Jefferson
in Communist attempts to capture him as their American
symbol. Ignoring his basic principle of individual freedom,
they have vainly tried to distort his social principle of
"utility to man" in a manner most repugnant to The Anti-
Totalitarian of Monticello, who had solemnly sworn and
had vigorously put into action on many fronts his "eternal
hostility against every form of tyranny."

"His history is indeed the history of American liberty,"
said Hugh Blair Grigsby. And so it is for his long years in
the public service. In his youth he successfully led a blood-
less social revolution in Virginia, embracing economic,
intellectual, and religious liberty. In the very last years of
his life, a gallant and indomitable "Old Sachem," he advocated a broad system of public education and established
a university "based on the illimitable freedom of the
human mind to explore and expose every subject." Always
he strove to attain his basic goals: the freedom and happiness of man. It was these goals, it was the "unchangeable
. . . inherent and inalienable rights of man," that were of

paramount importance. Decidedly secondary were the varied methods or weapons used to attain them. He strove mightily to attain the maximum of individual liberty, yet he was aware that man as a social creature must act through his government, local, state, and national. He was aware also that such slogans, often attributed to him, as "government is best when it governs least" and "power is always the enemy of liberty" must not be taken too literally. He himself had learned one lesson the hard way, as a not too successful war governor before becoming an effective President. It was that governmental power strongly asserted is often vital to win and to maintain liberty.

He changed his methods to meet particular problems. He employed the weapon most effective at the time to gain his liberal and humanitarian objectives, keeping in mind that majority rule is "the first principle of republicanism." Again and again Jefferson emphasized these basic ideas: "The Creator has made the earth for the living, not the dead." Changing conditions in a changing world will force each generation to change its methods, since "laws and institutions must go hand in hand . . . and keep pace with the times." But always and eternally unchangeable are man's inalienable rights and the selfsame democratic goals, man's freedom and happiness. And this is the hard core of his progressive democratic philosophy; its living, timeless essence; as applicable in our industrialized America as in his agrarian America.

Jefferson was the great democratic idealist, yet a practical and effective one. He was pragmatic, not dogmatic, a shrewd politician who well knew that in a free society politics is the art of the possible. He keenly realized that democracy is both a faith in man's capacity for self-government and an experimental process—a liberal procedure which combines fixed standards with flexibility, and avoids both radical and reactionary extremes. He called his elec-

tion "the revolution of 1800." On assuming office, however, he said he would of course "fall short of effecting all
the reformation" he desired. Knowing "how difficult it is
to move or inflect the great machine of society, how impossible to advance the notions of a whole people suddenly
to ideal right, we see the wisdom of Solon's remark that
no more good must be attempted than the nation can
bear." Yet with his habitual optimism he steadily and at
times very boldly pushed ahead on his course of enlightened liberalism. "Sensible that we are acting for all mankind," setting a hopeful example for oppressed peoples
everywhere, he was determined to advance as best he could
America's "interesting experiment of self-government,"
always "with a single and steadfast eye to the general
interest and happiness."

To achieve his goals he used the weapons of states rights
and of national rights. In 1798 he employed the Virginia
and Kentucky Resolutions, but not to exalt states rights as
such. He used them primarily as a weapon to defend basic
civil liberties violated by the Alien and Sedition Acts. As
President, in 1803 he purchased half a continent in the
Louisiana Territory, extending "our empire of liberty" in
a "transaction replete with blessings to unborn millions of
men." Here he boldly cast aside "metaphysical subtleties."
He wisely placed the national good above the strict con-
structionist view of the Constitution he had earlier used in
fighting Hamilton's fiscal policies. In 1806 he suggested a
national welfare program in which revenues from a continuing tariff would be spent for a national university and
a nation-wide network of canals and highways. In his
much-criticized Embargo Act of 1807 against the aggres-
sions of Britain and France, in an unprecedented manner,
unparalleled indeed until the Civil War, he exerted the
power of the nation's government for the nation's welfare
and security.

It was Pickering's Federalists who now upheld the laissez-faire, states rights position. They opposed the national government even more violently than the Jeffersonians did in the 1790s. Jefferson had so "out-Hamiltoned Alexander Hamilton" that John Randolph of Roanoke led the states rights extremists of his own party into opposition. Thenceforth doctrinaire John Randolph, darling of today's "New Conservatives," sneered at his cousin of Monticello as that hypocritical "St. Thomas of *Cantingbury*." He vilified him to the delight of his new Federalist friends. Timothy Pickering admitted that Randolph even outdid himself in vituperation. He wished the Virginian well when he swore to do all he could to make true his prediction that Jefferson's "character on the page of history will appear black as hell."

As "The Noble Agrarian" to many admirers, and as an ignoble one to the mercantile Federalists, he has long been over-simplified. Strong indeed were his loyalties to his Virginia planter's way of life and to that of America's farmers, who were then an overwhelming majority of the population. But as a public servant he strove to advance the economic interests of the whole nation. Federalist business men harshly denounced him as a doctrinaire agrarian, hell-bent with his Embargo on destroying their shipping and commerce. But a recent scholarly study more realistically calls him a "Commercial Agrarian Democrat." Early in his career he opposed manufacturing and, in words that are still twisted and distorted, "the mobs of great cities." But he wisely changed these earlier views, since America then lacked manufacturing sufficient even to equip her armies to fight the War of 1812. With his nail factory at Monticello he himself became in a small way a pioneer industrialist.

The uses and abuses of history are many, as The Strange Case of Thomas Jefferson abundantly illustrates. But most

persistent and flagrant of abuses are attempts rigorously to
limit his usefulness in time and place to the so-called "lost
world of Thomas Jefferson," the farmer-republic of an
earlier America. Nothing does greater injustice to him and
to "the sanctity of history" than to confuse the changing
methods he used in his generation with his unchangeable
democratic goals; or narrowly to equate his so-called "agrarian democracy" of a dead past with his fundamental principles that are universal, timeless, and very much alive.

He is today most appreciated because men are more
clearly informed as to his basic philosophy. They are more
keenly aware, as Benjamin Rush once said, that while
Washington fought and Patrick Henry talked, Jefferson
thought for the American Revolution. And the American
Revolution to Rush and to Jefferson was far more than a
war for independence. It is a continuing story both political and cultural, constantly evolving, with new chapters
written in each generation. It touches everything, Jefferson
believed, that gives promise of "enlightening the mind of
man, and improving him as a rational, moral, and social
being."

In our time, as in his, Jefferson has an especial appeal
for men of good minds and good hearts, who would have
their generation write as good a chapter as possible in this
unfolding story. They admire him not only for his progressive political thought and action, his robust and inspiring democratic faith, but for his many and diverse cultural
contributions. They appreciate him, and find him fascinat-
ing, in his roles as Scientist, Philosopher, Architect, Classi-
cist, Inventor, Farmer, Horticulturist, Bibliophile, Educa-
tor — the list seems endless. His versatility is suggested by
the some 10,000 entries in John P. Foley's *Jeffersonian
Cyclopedia,* where he ranges from "Academies" and "Art"
on and on to "Young Men" and "Zeal." When he speaks
of Young Men, Jefferson speaks of education and enthusi-

asm, of young men as preservers of the best in the past and the makers of a better world. And of Zeal, he speaks of its necessity in pursuing every good cause, undeterred by selfishness or ridicule. "I fear that my zeal will make me expose myself to ridicule," he wrote in this last entry, "but this risk becomes a duty by the bare possibility of doing good."

In his old age he himself selected only three of his many contributions to mankind to be inscribed on his tomb-stone at Monticello. All three are significant expressions of that basic social and political philosophy to which, risk-ing ridicule and vilification, he had through a long and fruitful life devoted his talents. All three deal with one thing: "Author of the Declaration of American Independ-ence" — political freedom; "Of the Statute of Virginia for Religious Freedom" — freedom of conscience; "And Father of the University of Virginia" — intellectual freedom, the most precious of all, as he said, because it safeguards all other freedoms. And that freedom-fighters of our day, at home and abroad, find in him a contemporary comrade-in-arms whose principles are still "the definitions and axioms of free society . . . applicable to all men and all times," brings to a happy ending this report on The Strange Case of Thomas Jefferson.

harper ✦ torchbooks

HUMANITIES AND SOCIAL SCIENCES

American Studies

JOHN R. ALDEN: The American Revolution, 1775-1783. *Illus.*   TB/3011

RAY A. BILLINGTON: The Far Western Frontier, 1830-1860. *Illus.*   TB/3012

RANDOLPH S. BOURNE: The War and the Intellectuals: *A Collection of Essays, 1915-1919. Edited with an Introduction by Carl Resek*   TB/3043

JOSEPH CHARLES: The Origins of the American Party System   TB/1049

T. C. COCHRAN & WILLIAM MILLER: The Age of Enterprise: *A Social History of Industrial America*   TB/1054

FOSTER RHEA DULLES: America's Rise to World Power, 1898-1954. *Illus.*   TB/3021

W. A. DUNNING: Reconstruction, Political and Economic, 1865-1877   TB/1073

CLEMENT EATON: The Growth of Southern Civilization, 1790-1860. *Illus.*   TB/3040

HAROLD U. FAULKNER: Politics, Reform and Expansion, 1890-1900. *Illus.*   TB/3020

LOUIS FILLER: The Crusade against Slavery, 1830-1860. *Illus.*   TB/3029

EDITORS OF FORTUNE: America in the Sixties: the Economy and the Society. *Two-color charts* TB/1015

LAWRENCE HENRY GIPSON: The Coming of the Revolution, 1763-1775. *Illus.*   TB/3007

FRANCIS J. GRUND: Aristocracy in America: *Jacksonian Democracy*   TB/1001

MARCUS LEE HANSEN: The Atlantic Migration: 1607-1860. *Edited by Arthur M. Schlesinger; Introduction by Oscar Handlin*   TB/1052

JOHN D. HICKS: Republican Ascendancy, 1921-1933.* *Illus.*   TB/3041

JOHN HIGHAM, Ed.: The Reconstruction of American History   TB/1068

ROBERT H. JACKSON: The Supreme Court in the American System of Government   TB/1106

WILLIAM E. LEUCHTENBURG: Franklin D. Roosevelt and the New Deal, 1932-1940. *Illus.*   TB/3025

LEONARD W. LEVY: Freedom of Speech and Press in Early American History: *Legacy of Suppression*   TB/1109

ARTHUR S. LINK: Woodrow Wilson and the Progressive Era, 1910-1917. *Illus.*   TB/3023

BERNARD MAYO: Myths and Men: *Patrick Henry, George Washington, Thomas Jefferson* TB/1108

JOHN C. MILLER: The Federalist Era, 1789-1801.*Illus.*   TB/3027

PERRY MILLER & T. H. JOHNSON, Editors: The Puritans: *A Sourcebook of Their Writings*
Volume I TB/1093
Volume II TB/1094

GEORGE E. MOWRY: The Era of Theodore Roosevelt and the Birth of Modern America, 1900-1912.*Illus.*   TB/3022

WALLACE NOTESTEIN: The English People on the Eve of Colonization, 1603-1630. *Illus.*   TB/3006

RUSSEL BLAINE NYE: The Cultural Life of the New Nation, 1776-1801. *Illus.*   TB/3026

GEORGE E. PROBST, Ed.: The Happy Republic: *A Reader in Tocqueville's America*   TB/1060

FRANK THISTLETHWAITE: America and the Atlantic Community: *Anglo-American Aspects, 1790-1850*   TB/1107

TWELVE SOUTHERNERS: I'll Take My Stand: *The South and the Agrarian Tradition. Introduction by Louis D. Rubin, Jr.; Biographical Essays by Virginia Rock*   TB/1072

A. F. TYLER: Freedom's Ferment: *Phases of American Social History from the Revolution to the Outbreak of the Civil War. Illus.*   TB/1074

GLYNDON G. VAN DEUSEN: The Jacksonian Era, 1828-1848. *Illus.*   TB/3028

WALTER E. WEYL: The New Democracy: *An Essay on Certain Political and Economic Tendencies in the United States*   TB/3042

LOUIS B. WRIGHT: The Cultural Life of the American Colonies, 1607-1763. *Illus.*   TB/3005

LOUIS B. WRIGHT: Culture on the Moving Frontier   TB/1053

Anthropology & Sociology

W. E. LE GROS CLARK: The Antecedents of Man: *An Introduction to the Evolution of the Primates. Illus.*   TB/559

ST. CLAIR DRAKE & HORACE R. CAYTON: Black Metropolis: *A Study of Negro Life in a Northern City. Introduction by Everett C. Hughes. Tables, maps, charts and graphs*
Volume I TB/1086
Volume II TB/1087

CORA DU BOIS: The People of Alor. *New Preface by the author. Illus.*
Volume I TB/1042
Volume II TB/1043

L. S. B. LEAKEY: Adam's Ancestors: *The Evolution of Man and his Culture. Illus.*   TB/1019

ROBERT H. LOWIE: Primitive Society. *Introduction by Fred Eggan*   TB/1056

TALCOTT PARSONS & EDWARD A. SHILS, Editors: Toward a General Theory of Action: *Theoretical Foundations for the Social Sciences*   TB/1083

SIR EDWARD TYLOR: The Origins of Culture. *Part I of "Primitive Culture." Introduction by Paul Radin*   TB/33

SIR EDWARD TYLOR: Religion in Primitive Culture. *Part II of "Primitive Culture." Introduction by Paul Radin*   TB/34

W. LLOYD WARNER: Social Class in America: *The Evaluation of Status*   TB/1013

Art and Art History

EMILE MÂLE: The Gothic Image: *Religious Art in France of the Thirteenth Century. 190 illus.*   TB/44

ERWIN PANOFSKY: Studies in Iconology: *Humanistic Themes in the Art of the Renaissance. 180 illustrations*   TB/1077

ALEXANDRE PIANKOFF: The Shrines of Tut-Ankh-Amon. *Edited by N. Rambova. 117 illus.*   TB/2011

*The New American Nation Series, edited by Henry Steele Commager and Richard B. Morris.

I

JEAN SEZNEC: The Survival of the Pagan Gods: *The Mythological Tradition and Its Place in Renaissance Humanism and Art*. 108 illustrations   TB/2004

HEINRICH ZIMMER: Myths and Symbols in Indian Art and Civilization. *70 illustrations*   TB/2005

Business, Economics & Economic History

REINHARD BENDIX: Work and Authority in Industry: *Ideologies of Management in the Course of Industrialization*   TB/3035

THOMAS C. COCHRAN: The American Business System: *A Historical Perspective, 1900-1955*   TB/1080

ROBERT DAHL & CHARLES E. LINDBLOM: Politics, Economics, and Welfare: *Planning and Politico-Economic Systems Resolved into Basic Social Processes*   TB/3037

PETER F. DRUCKER: The New Society: *The Anatomy of Industrial Order*   TB/1082

ROBERT L. HEILBRONER: The Great Ascent: *The Struggle for Economic Development*   TB/3030

PAUL MANTOUX: The Industrial Revolution in the Eighteenth Century: *The Beginnings of the Modern Factory System in England*   TB/1079

WILLIAM MILLER, Ed.: Men in Business: *Essays on the Historical Role of the Entrepreneur*   TB/1081

PERRIN STRYKER: The Character of the Executive: *Eleven Studies in Managerial Qualities*   TB/1041

PIERRE URI: Partnership for Progress.   TB/3036

Contemporary Culture

JACQUES BARZUN: The House of Intellect   TB/1051

JOHN U. NEF: Cultural Foundations of Industrial Civilization   TB/1024

PAUL VALÉRY: The Outlook for Intelligence   TB/2016

History: General

L. CARRINGTON GOODRICH: A Short History of the Chinese People. *Illus.*   TB/3015

DAN N. JACOBS & HANS BAERWALD: Chinese Communism: *Selected Documents*   TB/3031

BERNARD LEWIS: The Arabs in History   TB/1029

SIR PERCY SYKES: A History of Exploration. *Introduction by John K. Wright*   TB/1046

History: Ancient and Medieval

A. ANDREWES: The Greek Tyrants   TB/1103

HELEN CAM: England before Elizabeth   TB/1026

NORMAN COHN: The Pursuit of the Millennium: *Revolutionary Messianism in medieval and Reformation Europe and its bearing on modern totalitarian movements*   TB/1037

G. G. COULTON: Medieval Village, Manor, and Monastery   TB/1022

F. L. GANSHOF: Feudalism   TB/1058

J. M. HUSSEY: The Byzantine World   TB/1057

SAMUEL NOAH KRAMER: Sumerian Mythology   TB/1055

FERDINAND LOT: The End of the Ancient World and the Beginnings of the Middle Ages. *Introduction by Glanville Downey*   TB/1044

J. M. WALLACE-HADRILL: The Barbarian West: *The Early Middle Ages, A.D. 400-1000*   TB/1061

History: Renaissance & Reformation

JACOB BURCKHARDT: The Civilization of the Renaissance in Italy. *Introduction by Benjamin Nelson and Charles Trinkaus. Illus.*   Volume I TB/40
Volume II TB/41

ERNST CASSIRER: The Individual and the Cosmos in Renaissance Philosophy. *Translated with an Introduction by Mario Domandi*   TB/1097

EDWARD P. CHEYNEY: The Dawn of a New Era, *1250-1453* †*Illus.*   TB/3002

WALLACE K. FERGUSON, et al.: Facets of the Renaissance   TB/1098

WALLACE K. FERGUSON, et al.: The Renaissance: *Six Essays. Illus.*   TB/1084

MYRON P. GILMORE: The World of Humanism, *1453-1517.* †*Illus.*   TB/3003

JOHAN HUIZINGA: Erasmus and the Age of Reformation. *Illus.*   TB/19

PAUL O. KRISTELLER: Renaissance Thought: *The Classic, Scholastic, and Humanist Strains*   TB/1048

NICCOLÒ MACHIAVELLI: History of Florence and of the Affairs of Italy: *from the earliest times to the death of Lorenzo the Magnificent. Introduction by Felix Gilbert*   TB/1027

ALFRED VON MARTIN: Sociology of the Renaissance. *Introduction by W. K. Ferguson*   TB/1099

J. E. NEALE: The Age of Catherine de Medici   TB/1085

ERWIN PANOFSKY: Studies in Iconology: *Humanistic Themes in the Art of the Renaissance. 180 illustrations*   TB/1077

J. H. PARRY: The Establishment of the European Hegemony: *1415-1715: Trade and Exploration in the Age of the Renaissance*   TB/1045

HENRI PIRENNE: Early Democracies in the Low Countries: *Urban Society and Political Conflict in the Middle Ages and the Renaissance. Introduction by John H. Mundy*   TB/1110

FERDINAND SCHEVILL: The Medici. *Illus.*   TB/1010

FERDINAND SCHEVILL: Medieval and Renaissance Florence. *Illus.* Volume I: *Medieval Florence*   TB/1090
Volume II: *The Coming of Humanism and the Age of the Medici*   TB/1091

G. M. TREVELYAN: England in the Age of Wycliffe, *1368-1520*   TB/1112

VESPASIANO: Renaissance Princes, Popes, and Prelates: *The Vespasiano Memoirs: Lives of Illustrious Men of the XVth Century. Introduction by Myron P. Gilmore. Illus.*   TB/1111

History: Modern European

FREDERICK B. ARTZ: Reaction and Revolution, *1815-1832.* †*Illus.*   TB/3034

MAX BELOFF: The Age of Absolutism, *1660-1815*   TB/1062

ROBERT C. BINKLEY: Realism and Nationalism, *1852-1871.* †*Illus.*   TB/3038

CRANE BRINTON: A Decade of Revolution, *1789-1799.* †*Illus.*   TB/3018

J. BRONOWSKI & BRUCE MAZLISH: The Western Intellectual Tradition: *From Leonardo to Hegel*   TB/3001

GEOFFREY BRUUN: Europe and the French Imperium, *1799-1814.* †*Illus.*   TB/3033

WALTER L. DORN: Competition for Empire, *1740-1763.* †*Illus.*   TB/3032

CARL J. FRIEDRICH: The Age of the Baroque, *1610-1660.* †*Illus.*   TB/3004

LEO GERSHOY: From Despotism to Revolution, *1763-1789.* †*Illus.*   TB/3017

†*The Rise of Modern Europe Series*, edited by **William L. Langer.**

3

NATURAL SCIENCES AND MATHEMATICS

Biological Sciences

Chemistry

Geography

History of Science

Mathematics

WILLARD VAN ORMAN QUINE: Mathematical Logic
TB/558
O. G. SUTTON: Mathematics in Action. *Foreword by James R. Newman. Illus.* TB/518
FREDERICK WAISMANN: Introduction to Mathematical Thinking. *Foreword by Karl Menger* TB/511

Philosophy of Science

R. B. BRAITHWAITE: Scientific Explanation TB/515
J. BRONOWSKI: Science and Human Values. *Illus.* TB/505
ALBERT EINSTEIN: Philosopher-Scientist. *Edited by Paul A. Schilpp* Volume I TB/502
Volume II TB/503
WERNER HEISENBERG: Physics and Philosophy: *The Revolution in Modern Science. Introduction by F. S. C. Northrop* TB/549
JOHN MAYNARD KEYNES: A Treatise on Probability. *Introduction by N. R. Hanson* TB/557
STEPHEN TOULMIN: Foresight and Understanding: *An Enquiry into the Aims of Science. Foreword by Jacques Barzun* TB/564
STEPHEN TOULMIN: The Philosophy of Science: *An Introduction* TB/513
W. H. WATSON: On Understanding Physics. *Introduction by Ernest Nagel* TB/507
G. J. WHITROW: The Natural Philosophy of Time
TB/563

Physics and Cosmology

DAVID BOHM: Causality and Chance in Modern Physics. *Foreword by Louis de Broglie* TB/536
P. W. BRIDGMAN: The Nature of Thermodynamics
TB/537
LOUIS DE BROGLIE: Physics and Microphysics. *Foreword by Albert Einstein* TB/514
T. G. COWLING: Molecules in Motion: *An Introduction to the Kinetic Theory of Gases. Illus.* TB/516
A. C. CROMBIE, Ed.: Turning Point in Physics TB/535
C. V. DURELL: Readable Relativity. *Foreword by Freeman J. Dyson* TB/530
ARTHUR EDDINGTON: Space, Time and Gravitation: *An outline of the General Relativity Theory* TB/510
GEORGE GAMOW: Biography of Physics TB/567
MAX JAMMER: Concepts of Force: *A Study in the Foundation of Dynamics* TB/550
MAX JAMMER: Concepts of Space: *The History of Theories of Space in Physics. Foreword by Albert Einstein* TB/533
EDMUND WHITTAKER: History of the Theories of Aether and Electricity
Volume I: *The Classical Theories* TB/531
Volume II: *The Modern Theories* TB/532
G. J. WHITROW: The Structure and Evolution of the Universe: *An Introduction to Cosmology. Illus.*
TB/504

A LETTER TO THE READER

Overseas, there is considerable belief
that we are a country of extreme conservatism and
that we cannot accommodate to social change.

Books about America in the hands of
readers abroad can help change those ideas.

The U. S. Information Agency cannot,
by itself, meet the vast need for books about
the United States.

You can help.

Harper Torchbooks provides three packets
of books on American history, economics,
sociology, literature and politics to
help meet the need.

To send a packet of Torchbooks (retailing
at $10.85 to $12.00) overseas, all you need
do is send your check for $7 (which includes
cost of shipping) to Harper & Row. The U. S.
Information Agency will distribute the books
to libraries, schools, and other centers
all over the world.

I ask every American to support this
program, part of a worldwide BOOKS USA campaign.

I ask you to share in the opportunity to
help tell others about America.

EDWARD R. MURROW
Director,
U. S. Information Agency

PACKET I: *Twentieth Century America*

Dulles/America's Rise to World Power, 1898-1954
Cochran/The American Business System, 1900-1955
Zabel, Editor/Literary Opinion in America (two volumes)
Drucker/The New Society: *The Anatomy of Industrial Order*
Fortune Editors/America in the Sixties: *The Economy and the Society*

PACKET II: *American History*

Billington/The Far Western Frontier, 1830-1860
Mowry/The Era of Theodore Roosevelt and the
   Birth of Modern America, 1900-1912
Faulkner/Politics, Reform, and Expansion, 1890-1900
Cochran & Miller/The Age of Enterprise: *A Social History of
   Industrial America*
Tyler/Freedom's Ferment: *American Social History from the
   Revolution to the Civil War*

PACKET III: *American History*

Hansen/The Atlantic Migration, 1607-1860
Degler/Out of Our Past: *The Forces that Shaped Modern America*
Probst, Editor/The Happy Republic: *A Reader in Tocqueville's America*
Alden/The American Revolution, 1775-1783
Wright/The Cultural Life of the American Colonies, 1607-1763

*Your gift will be acknowledged directly to you by the overseas recipient.
Simply fill out the coupon, detach and mail with your check or money order.*

HARPER & ROW, PUBLISHERS · BOOKS USA DEPT.
49 East 33rd Street, New York 16, N. Y.

Packet I ☐   Packet II ☐   Packet III ☐

Please send the BOOKS USA library packet(s) indicated above, in my
name, to the area checked below. Enclosed is my remittance in the
amount of _____ for _____ packet(s) at $7.00 each.

_____ Africa   _____ Latin America

_____ Far East   _____ Near East

Name_____

Address_____

_____

NOTE: This offer expires December 31, 1966.